SACRED SEX

SACRED SEX

EROTIC WRITINGS FROM
THE RELIGIONS OF THE WORLD

Robert Bates

Fount
An Imprint of HarperCollins*Publishers*

Fount Paperbacks is an Imprint of
HarperCollins*Religious*
Part of HarperCollins*Publishers*
77–85 Fulham Palace Road,
Hammersmith, London W6 8JB

First published in Great Britain
in 1993 by Fount Paperbacks

1 3 5 7 9 10 8 6 4 2

A catalogue record for this book is
available from the British Library

ISBN 0 00 627686 5

Typeset by Whitelaw & Palmer Ltd, Glasgow

Printed and bound in Great Britain by
HarperCollinsManufacturing Glasgow

CONTENTS

INTRODUCTION

Sex is the point where the spiritual and the physical aspects of human experience are most closely inter-woven. A person who is afraid of their own inner feelings and emotions may wish that casual intercourse could be a purely physical activity, like eating a cream cake. But, like it or not, emotions soon intervene: sex without love becomes tasteless, even disgusting, and may eventually become physically impossible. Equally a person who is afraid of physical intimacy may imagine that their sexual desires can be ignored, or be elevated and transformed into spiritual feelings. But without any honest expression of sexual desire, frustration can overwhelm the human psyche, filling the heart with anger and resentment.

So from the earliest times the various religions of the world, concerned with humankind's spiritual needs, have focused on sex. In every culture religion has sought to impose order on sexual relationships, prescribing who may have sexual intercourse with whom – and also what sexual relationships are forbidden. A taboo on incest – sex between close relations – is universal across the world, although societies vary in their precise definition of incest:

some cultures, for example, allow sex between first cousins, while others may regard sex even between second and third cousins as an abomination. Similarly every culture has some form of marriage, and hence some notion of adultery. Even a polygamous system of marriage – in which one man may have many wives, or, in rare instances, where one woman has many husbands (polyandry) – must be upheld by strict rules preventing intercourse outside the marital bond.

The religions of the world have also recognized that people need sexual guidance, to attain lasting fulfilment. Sex offers the most intense joy that any human being can experience, yet it is also the aspect of life most fraught with anxiety. Thus religious teachers have made it their business to turn anxiety into joy. The sex manuals which now festoon our bookshops are inferior imitations of the wonderfully imaginative sexual guides which have been produced by priests and gurus over the past three thousand years. The modern manual, devoid of any spiritual context, reduces sex to a matter of technique. The religious manuals are equally explicit, yet emphasize sexual artistry and tenderness. And they pay particular attention to sexual problems – staleness, impotency, premature ejaculation and so on – which can be such a source of misery, offering methods of cure.

Despite the strength of the sexual urge, most men and women have always spent part of their lives without sexual partners. In teenage years there is usually a significant gap between puberty and full sexual activity; and in societies under constant danger of war, young men have often been required to delay marriage and sex until their mid or late twenties, in order to serve as warriors. In many periods of history there has been a substantial imbalance between the numbers of men and women, so that many of one sex are left unmarried; and even where there is balance, people may be slow to find a partner. And in later years premature death of a partner can foreshorten sexual activity. In addition there have also been those who actually wish to remain celibate. Yet celibacy does not, and should not, imply the denial of sexuality. There is a wealth of highly emotive religious literature in which the sexual instinct is channelled, quite honestly and openly, towards divine contemplation. This literature can, of course, be enjoyed by people who are sexually active. But in Hinduism and Islam, as well as in Christianity, men and women have always recognized that celibacy, when linked with deep religious devotion, can bring true sexual fulfilment.

In modern Western society sexual attitudes and behaviour are in a state of profound confusion and change. Lifelong monogamy, in which a man and a woman remain sexually faithful until death, has for many centuries been the moral norm; and, judging by popular music and romantic fiction, it remains the ideal to which most aspire. Yet in practice many, perhaps most, partnerships are broken before death, and it is now quite common for a person to have a series of partnerships over the course of a lifetime. And short, even casual, sexual relationships no longer provoke the moral outrage of the past. At the same time, sexual expectations are higher than ever. Fifty or a hundred years ago sexual pleasure was widely regarded, especially by women, as the brief, transient reward of youth; but after the first blissful months of marriage – and especially after the first pregnancy – most were resigned to sex becoming a perfunctory, joyless affair. Today, however, middle-aged and even elderly people seek the same degree of sexual pleasure as newlyweds; and sexual failure in a partnership is regarded either as a problem to be solved, or as cause for breaking the bond.

The ancient sexual teaching resolves the confusions and meets the expectations. Every religion teaches that sex only brings fulfilment if it is within the context of a loving – and a faithful – relationship. Fidelity is prescribed not only for moral reasons, but because sustained sexual pleasure requires a couple to feel secure in their intimacy, and thus able to give themselves fully and without inhibition to one another. Indeed many sexual problems, including impotency and frigidity, are seen as largely deriving from anxiety and insecurity, and thus can only be overcome within a relationship of total mutual acceptance. Most religious teachers on sexuality recognize that relationships can fail, and then should be allowed to break apart peaceably. Yet they speak almost as one in regarding lifelong faithfulness as the best foundation for sexual enjoyment.

The purpose of the religious sexual manuals, therefore, was to enable couples to continue enjoying sex throughout their lives. The audience for whom they were written was not pubescent boys and girls, or even young men and women embarking on marriage. The energy of youth makes sex lively and enjoyable without any special skills. But as the years pass a couple should learn more subtle artistry if the sexual flame is to keep burning. The middle-aged and elderly couple must become more sensitive to each other's needs and more varied in their technique, and they must learn to conserve their sexual powers. Couples in their 40s, 50s, 60s, and 70s – and even older – can derive even greater sexual enjoyment than young people, if together they practise the ancient wisdom of Hinduism, Buddhism, Taoism and Islam.

This book is the first collection of erotic spiritual writings from across the world. Every major religion is represented, as are the ancient religions of Egypt, Greece and Rome; in addition two tribal religions, whose erotic stories and poems have been written down, are included. There is a wide variation in style and approach, yet they fall into three main categories. The first is where sexual feelings are spiritualized and directed to the divinity. Christianity has the richest tradition of this form of sexual prayer, but Hindu love of Krishna and the Islamic prayers to the 'Beloved' are also highly erotic. The second is the literature of lovers, in which their mutual attraction is a metaphor of religious devotion. Judaism and Egyptian religion have especially beautiful examples of this. The third and most important is where religious teachers directly address the subject of sex. There is a poetic beauty about these ancient erotic writings which is absent in modern secular books and videos about sex; and yet the ancient works are as explicit as anything on the bookshelves today.

Since this collection is offered to the general reader, rather than to the scholar, a certain amount of editing has been necessary, to avoid needless repetition. The three major Hindu manuals of sex, for example, contain a number of almost identical chapters; so the first manual, the *Kama Sutra*, is given most fully, while only the fresh material from the later manuals is included. Equally the great Islamic verses addressing the Beloved can become very tedious in large quantities, since many of the poems are very similar; but careful pruning much increases the reader's enjoyment.

At first sight it may seem shocking, especially for a Christian reader, to find Teresa of Avila and St John of the Cross rubbing shoulders with the *Kama Sutra* and *The Perfumed Garden*. And the couple seeking practical sexual guidance may see little point in reading the erotic mystical poetry of Hafiz or Vidyapati. Yet taken together the writings contained in this book are a wonderful testimony to the range, the power and the beauty of human sexual experience. This book is a celebration of the sexual instinct which can both inspire the loftiest prayer and yield the most intense pleasure.

SACRED SEX

HINDUISM

INTRODUCTION: HINDUISM

Of all the major religions, Hinduism gives the greatest importance to sex. Sexual pleasure is regarded as one of the four basic objectives of human life, the others being material wealth, spiritual salvation, and moral duty. Thus the famous sex manuals of India, teaching the art of sexual enjoyment, are treated as sacred texts. Moreover the sexual union of men and women is frequently used by mystics and poets as a metaphor for the union between God and the human soul. At the same time Hinduism teaches that the soul which truly seeks divine union must free itself from all bodily attachments, including sexual desire. And to this day many Hindus still follow the ancient laws of Manu, which require that in middle age men and women should gradually reduce their sexual activity, until as celibates they devote themselves wholly to religion.

This ambivalent attitude to sex is most clearly expressed in Siva, one of the two major Hindu gods. His symbol is the phallus or "lingam", and he is regarded as the god of sexual pleasure. When he fell in love with Parvati, a beautiful young goddess, the friction generated by their love-play shook the entire universe; and so great was the heat within Parvati's 'yoni' that it caught fire, and ashes fell to the earth. So there are numerous shrines both to Siva's lingam and to Parvati's yoni. At the same time Siva is the god of asceticism, worshipped by men and women vowed to celibacy. After his affair with Parvati, Siva lived as a hermit in the forest, causing his sexual potency to become spiritual power; and it is this power which enables ordinary humans to free themselves from bodily attachments.

Vishnu, the second major god, became incarnate in the dark, handsome figure of Krishna, who also combines austerity with sexual activity. In some texts he is a lofty teacher of morality, urging the strictest standards of behaviour. But in other texts he is a young cowherd seducing beautiful girls. His particular favourite is Radha, with whom he disappears into the forest to make love. As a result a number of fine religious poets identified with Radha, expressing their spiritual yearning for God in the form of highly erotic poetry.

When Europeans began to come to India in large numbers in the eighteenth century, the Indians were contemptuous of their sexual incompetence, calling them 'dung-hill cocks'. Sexual intercourse for the Europeans was a hurried, shameful business, devoid of spiritual grace. And since they knew only one postion, with the man on top, this became known as the 'missionary position', after the Christian missionaries were spotted practising it. Indians by contrast had for generations enjoyed the benefits of beautiful and explicit sex manuals, dedicated to Kama, the god of pleasure. These teach not only a wide variety of positions for intercourse itself, but also every other aspect of lovemaking; and they urge men and women to have pride, not shame, in their sexual activities, since the joy of sex reflects the joy of divine union. The later sex manuals were also aimed at married couples whose love had grown stale: by learning more varied and sophisticated sexual acts the passion of youth could be restored.

The sacredness of sex is most vividly expressed in Hindu art. The teachings of the sex manuals are illustrated in numerous paintings which, far from being shocking, have a wonderful charm and even innocence. More particularly many Hindu temples show gods and goddesses in sexual union.

BHAGAVATA PURRANA

O ne of the central figures in Hindu religious stories is Krishna, meaning 'the dark one,' an incarnation of the god Vishnu. Sometimes he appears as a solemn figure offering wise spiritual teaching. At others he is a handsome and sexy young cowherd. At one level this famous story of Krishna stealing the cowgirls' clothes is intended simply to illustrate his playful character – and hence the playfulness of the god Vishnu. At another level it is a divine parable: by forcing the girls to reveal their nakedness, he is demanding that people come spiritually naked before God; and he symbolically makes them submit to his divine power.

Krishna and the Girls' Clothes

In the first month of winter, the girls of the village of Gokula performed an act of worship to the goddess Katyayani. They ate rice cooked with ghee; they bathed at sunrise in the Kalindi river; they made an image of the goddess out of clay, decorating it with garlands of flowers, and placing around it sweet-smelling herbs. And, bowing their heads, they each prayed: 'Goddess Katyayani, make Krishna, the son of the cowherd Nanda, my husband.' Every day for a month the girls repeated these actions, and every day their hearts would grow in love for Krishna.

One morning, when they had taken off their clothes and were bathing joyfully in the river Kalindi, they all began to sing of Krishna, extolling his great beauty. Unknown to them, Krishna came to the river bank, took their clothes, and quickly climbed a Nipa tree, whose branches were heavy with fragrant orange blossom. Krishna then laughed loudly and called out: 'Girls, let each one of you come over here and take her clothes. You may come one by one, or all together.'

When the girls saw Krishna, and realized what his game was, they were overwhelmed with love for him. But they looked at one another in embarrassment, and refused to come out of the water. Instead they sank into it up to their necks, and began shivering with cold. 'You should not have played such a wicked trick,' they cried. 'You, the son of Nanda the cowherd, are the pride of our village, its most handsome young man. Give us back our clothes, so we can dress and become warm again. We are your slaves and will do what you command. But you must do your duty, otherwise we will tell your father.'

Krishna replied: 'If you are my slaves and will do as I command, then come here and take back your clothes.' So all the girls, trembling with cold, rose out of the water, covering their sexual parts with their hands. Krishna was pleased to see their slim naked bodies, and climbed down the tree with their clothes on his shoulder. As they approached him, he smiled and said: 'It was an insult to the goddess Katyayani to swim naked as part of your worship of her. So you must put your hands above your heads and then bow low in expiation for your sin. Then I will let you have your clothes.'

The girls believed that what Krishna was saying must be true, since they regarded him as infallible. So they put their hands above their heads and bowed low before him, kissing his feet. Krishna now felt pity for them, and gave them their clothes. Although Krishna had robbed them of their modesty and had mocked and tricked them, they held no grudge against him, because they were happy to be in his presence. As they put on their clothes, they could not help staring at him, their eyes filled with love.

Krishna said to them: 'Good ladies, I know that you desire to worship me. I rejoice in this desire, which deserves to be fulfilled. The desire for me does not give rise to further desire, just as seed corn which has been boiled or fried does not give rise to seed. Instead by worshipping me your desire will be satisfied and your hearts will be at peace. Now go back to your village, and each night you will enjoy me.'

The girls, in obedience to their beloved, forced themselves to leave him, and went back to their village.

VIDYAPATI

Recognized as one of the finest Hindu love poets, his verses are almost entirely concerned with the relationship between Krishna and his favourite cowgirl Radha, symbolizing the love between God and the individual. Vidyapati lived in northeastern India, and began his career as a poet at the king's court. But he soon grew weary of the luxurious life, and retired to a small hut near his native village, where he lived as a hermit. He died in about the year 1450, reputedly aged 100.

Emerging from Childhood

Radha's eyes darted from side to side.
Her body was restless and her clothes twitched.
She smiled nervously, her ivory teeth glistening.
Looking in the mirror she raised her skirt,
To see her body which yearned for love.
Each day she looked at her swelling breasts,
Feeling strange and awkward at such a strange sight.
Childhood melted into womanhood.
The new absorbed the old.

A Shapely Young Woman

Each day the breasts of Radha swelled.
Her hips grew wider, her waist more slender.
The secrets of love now filled her mind
And the emotions of childhood melted away.
Her firm breasts ached for love.
Krishna saw her as she bathed,
Her wet clothes clinging to her body,
To reveal to him her perfect form.
Beneath her dress she glowed like gold.

First Love

Her low voice trembled with fear and passion.
She was too shy to find words.
Now she seemed to consent, now she drew back.
When he asked for love, she closed her eyes.
He begged her for a kiss;
She turned her mouth away,
But his hand turned her face to his.
She felt her dress fall from her body,
She knew he was robbing love's treasure.

Krishna's Promise

As she awoke she could hear his voice.
He was whispering earnestly in her ear.
'Listen, sweet and lovely darling,
Do not feel angry at what I have done.

I promise by the beauty of your body
Which I have gathered in my hands,
That I will never touch anyone but you.
If my words prove false,
May your breasts ooze poison as I suck them,
May your kisses choke me to death.'

Radha's Confusion

Radha looked away from her lover,
And in low tones of anguish she spoke.
'Is this real or a dream?
I felt a river floooding my heart
When my lover devoured me.
I felt the sky fall upon me,
When my dress fell to the ground.
I felt the judder of an earthquake
When my lover fondled my breasts.
I felt bees buzzing round my mouth,
When my lover kissed me.
I am young and cannot resist his strength,
The violence of his passion overwhelms me.
He crushes my frail body
Like a wild animal crushing a flower.
Never have I know such pain.
Never have I known such joy.'

Krishna's Plea

'Your breasts are like golden cups.
Your glances are darts of love.
O beautiful one, protest no longer.
Like a bee buzzing around a bright flower,
I am hungry for the sweetness of your love.
Do not be cruel to me, I beg you.
Have pity on me in my desire.
No more can I suffer the agony of love.'

Radha's Ploy

'When my lover comes to my courtyard,
I shall smile demurely, and move away.
Frantic with love, he will snatch at my dress,
But I will not relent.
When he begs me for love
I shall smile but not speak.
When he reaches for my bodice
I shall push away his hand,
And I will scold him with my eyes.
Distraught, my beautiful bee will seize my chin,
And suck honey from my lips.
I shall have no strength to resist.'

Radha's Submission

'All doubts are gone.
The birds may sing a million songs,
A million moons may shine now.
When he is close to me,
My heart sings and my body shines.
Lift up my dress, beautiful lover,
And fill me with pure gold.
You are my shelter in the rain,
My ferry-boat across the river,
My warm fire in the cold weather,
My southern breeze in the summer heat.
Nobody else I need,
Only you.'

Radha's Joy

A friend came to see Radha,
Concerned about her condition.
Radha, pale with love, spoke freely.
'In talk love always grows,
But I cannot exaggerate this love.
It is greater than the world itself.
It is new, and shall always remain new.
Nothing can quench its leaping flames.
Since I was born I have dreamt of him.
In my imagination I have seen his beauty.
His gentle voice has always brushed my ears.
Nights with him pass by in seconds,
So ecstatic is my joy.

He plays the game of love
With divine skill and artistry.
I have held him in my heart
For millions upon millions of years.
In every former life since time began
He has been with me.
He shall remain with me in every future life.
The love which others enjoy
Is just a fleeting moment of pleasure.
My love will last for ever
Because my lover is divine.'

Radha's Stubbornness

In her heart Radha belonged to Krishna.
But in her mind she still resisted him.
She longed to welcome him night and day,
Yet after the early weeks of joy
She began to turn him away.
Krishna pined for her.
He could not sleep, and never lay down.
In the dark night he wandered alone,
Through the forests and over the mountain,
His head drooping with sadness.
He looked at other young women,
Hoping his love would turn to them.
But in every face he saw Radha's face,
In every smile was Radha's smile.
He refused to eat and his body wasted away.
The doctors tried to cure him with medicines,

But nothing could relieve his gloom.
The only medicine that could save him
Was the nectar of Radha's lips.

Radha's Grief

When Kirshna no longer came
Radha herself sank into a pit of gloom.
She wondered if Krishna no longer loved her,
If his heart had been stolen by another.
She thought he had forgotten her,
That her name was no longer on his lips.
And yet she hoped with all her heart
That he would return.
Around her bed she wove a garland of flowers,
And sprinkled upon her bed the sweetest perfume,
Praying that once again it would be his bed of love.
At times she felt angry at his desertion.
At times she repented her foolish pride.
'If he comes, I will give myself totally,
Never again shall I hold myself back.'

Radha's Fear

One moonlit night Krishna returned,
Hoping that his beloved would now receive him.
Her heart leapt with joy at the sight of her lover.
She beckoned him to her home.
He asked for her lips; but she turned away.
He touched her breast; but she jumped back.

Her desire was overwhelmed with fear.
She wanted his love with all her heart,
But she was frightened of his power.
She wanted to submit,
But could not bear to be his slave.

Ecstasy

Krishna sat and waited.
He looked longingly at her face and body.
She looked up and smiled faintly.
He smiled, his eyes aglow with love.
The force of love rose within her.
Her thighs trembled, her breasts swelled.
He leaned forward and stroked her hair.
Sweat began to glisten on her face.
His hand clasped her neck.
Suddenly she gave way.
Her face fell upon his.
She pressed her lips against his.
She pushed her breasts onto his chest.
He drank from her lips.
Then he gently untied her dress.
Her body melted at his touch.
No longer could she check her passion.

Aftermath

Her eyes drooped with sleep.
Her limbs were heavy with fatigue.

Her face and lips were drained of colour.
Her breasts and buttocks were soft.
All passion was spent.
Love was satisfied.
Her dreams were in heaven.

MIRABAI

From her earliest years this peasant girl from the desert of northwestern India wanted Krishna as her husband. As a young adult she left home to seek him by living alone in a mountain cave. Eventually Krishna came to her in a vision, and continued to visit her for many years. Her passionate and vivid poems record their encounters on the mountain. Since her death in the late sixteenth century she has become one of the most popular Hindu poets.

Frenzy

My Lord beat out a rhythm on the drums
And I danced before him, swaying to his beat.
As I danced I went into a frenzy.
I became mad with love, overcome with desire.
My Lord stopped beating, and handed me a cup.
I drank from it, rolling the liquid in my mouth.
Never have I tasted such intense sweetness.
My whole body became intensely hot,
And I collapsed to the ground.
I lay there, open to the love of my Lord.

Purity

I saw the dark clouds burst above me.
Water tumbled down upon me.
It rained and rained for two hours.
I lay shivering with cold, every garment soaked.
My Lord was washing me, cleansing me,
So that in purity I could receive him.
Then the rain stopped, and I heard a distant noise.
Tambourines rattled, and flutes played.
I knew that my Lord was returning;
Soon he would be here, dark and handsome.
I belonged to him, and he to me.
No-one could deny our love.

Submission

My Lord knelt beside me, and lifted my head.
I spoke to him in low, soft tones.
'Do not leave me here; take me with you.
I will endure hunger and exhaustion for you.
If you want my dress to be red, it shall be so.
If you want it yellow, it shall be so.
If you want my hair draped with pearls, it shall be so.
If you want my hair wild and dishevelled, it shall be so.
I am yours, and will do and be what you wish.'

Promise

My Lord smiled at me, and stroked my face.
His eyes moved down me, from my head to my feet,
And then he looked into my eyes.
'I shall not leave you here wet and cold.
I pushed you into a frenzy to open your heart to me.
Then I gave you the wine of love to drink.
I sent rain upon you to purify you,
And to test the warmth of your love.
Though your body was cold, your heart remained hot.
You shall be mine for ever.
I will love you until you are pale with exhaustion.
I will love you until you are wrinkled with age.
I will love you in this life and the next.
Nothing will assuage my love.'

Fulfilment

So my Lord took me to his realm,
Where death is afraid to go,
Where golden birds fly overhead
And fish swim in azure lakes,
Where trees bear blossom of pink and white,
Where the grass is soft and lush.
Our clothes dissolved into the air.
We lay naked on the grass.
Blossoms fell on our bodies as a fragrant blanket.
Fish jumped in the water to watch us.
Birds sang sweet chants to arouse us.

We loved fully, passionately, eternally.
Life was complete, life is complete.

SURDAS

Blind from birth, he grew into a morose young man obsessed with the spiritual gulf between himself and God. Then a wandering sage came to his village in northwestern India, and taught him to use his natural emotions and passions as the means of reaching God. He was soon pouring his feelings into poetry which, like that of Vidyapati, extolled the love of Krishna and Radha. He is said to have lived for 125 years, dying in 1715.

Krishna's Beauty

Look at Krishna's nimble eyes,
They shimmer like the scales of fish.
They dart this way and that like a swallow.
Who can resist their glance?
Who will not melt with love
When their eyes meet the eyes of Krishna?
Look at Krishna's noble body.
His muscles are like taut rope.
His legs are swift as a stallion's.
Who can resist his beauty?

Who will not melt with love
When their body touches the body of Krishna?

Radha's Confusion

He loves her, but she cannot believe it.
She is struck dumb by his words of love.
Her face is paralysed by his smile.
Her gaze is fixed on his gentle face.
Her brain is trapped by mental confusion.
'Does he love me, or is this a dream?'
He draws closer and touches her cheek.
She can feel the warmth of his palm.
Her body starts to fill with pleasure.
But again she is trapped by confusion.
'Does he love me, an ordinary mortal?
Or does he love every girl he sees?
Is love just a game he plays?
Or will he truly give me his heart?'

Fleeing from Love

Radha turns, and flees to the forest.
On each tree she rests her head
And weeps until the bark is moist.
Her tears dribble down through the branches of the tree
To water the roots below.
'I want this love beyond all the world.
But can I trust him? Is he faithful?
Or will he love me and discard me?

Am I like a nut in the mouth of a bird?
Will he consume my heart and spit out my body
Like a useless, tasteless shell?'

Fearing God

A person in love never thinks of death;
They imagine life and love will last for ever.
A person in love never flinches with pain;
Like a moth they fly eagerly at the flame.
A person in love never fears disaster;
Like a dove they fly as high as their strength allows.
But that was not Radha's way.
She loved a god, not a man.
She feared that love would destroy her.
She feared that she would be burnt up in its flame.
She feared her heart would plunge lifeless to earth.
So she fled from love.

Submitting to God

No human can defy a god.
Krishna pursued her and caught her.
When she heard his footsteps, she lifted her face.
She could not stop herself looking at him.
With his eyes he penetrated her breast,
And he stole her treasure, her heart.
With his words he penetrated her mind,
And he stole her thoughts, her will.
With his love he penetrated her body,

And he stole her virtue, her youth.
Krishna made Radha his own.
Love conquered fear.

Marks upon God

After a night and day of love,
Krishna and Radha lay down to sleep.
The shape of Radha's necklace was etched on his chest.
Her hair was on his clothes.
Marks of her teeth were on his shoulders.
Marks of her nails were on his back.
His body was bruised with her passionate embraces.
A god wears the signs of those who love him.

KAMA SUTRA

The most famous sex manual in the world, it was composed some time between the first and fourth centuries by a religious sage called Vatsyayana. He himself made no claim to originality, but was distilling the sexual teaching which he had learnt from earlier sages. And at the end of the work he wrote that he had tested the truth of the teaching through divine contemplation. The book was probably translated into Persian and Arabic in the medieval period, and so enjoyed wide circulation throughout the Islamic world. In the nineteenth century it was translated into English and thence to other European languages, since when it has had a profound influence on Western sexual attitudes.

Divine Laws

In the beginning the Lord of the Universe created men and women. And he ordained that they should live in accordance with three sets of laws. The first concerns moral virtue, through which humans can attain eternal bliss. The second concerns the acquisition of wealth –

land, gold, cattle and tools – through which bodily comfort is obtained. The third concerns the pleasures of the senses – hearing, feeling, seeing, tasting and smelling – by which life on earth is enjoyed. The greatest pleasure of the senses is that enjoyed through sexual union; and the laws concerning sexual activity are the subject of this treatise.

Some object that since sexual activity is practised by every creature on earth, prompted only by instinct, there is no need for any rules to govern it. This view is wrong. Amongst animals coitus is undertaken without prior thought, and the females are only able to have coitus at certain seasons. As a result little pleasure is obtained from it. Amongst humans, by contrast, sexual activity can give great pleasure if men and women reflect carefully on how best to conduct their sexual relations. And since women are capable of coitus at all seasons, it can be enjoyed continually. For these reasons the Lord of the Universe, who rejoices in our joy, has given us laws to guide sexual activity, and by studying these laws carefully, and applying them, our pleasure shall be complete.

It is also objected that, since divine destiny governs all things, we should not exert ourselves to acquire either wealth or pleasure. This too is wrong. Human exertion is itself part of destiny, and so to fail to exert himself a man is defying his destiny. It is the divine destiny of every man and woman to enjoy great sexual pleasure. So those who fail to exert themselves in learning to apply the laws of pleasure will fail to fulfil this destiny.

A third objection is that pleasure should not be sought, since it is an obstacle in the practice of moral virtue; and since moral virtue brings eternal bliss, while pleasure brings only temporary happiness, we should deny ourselves pleasure. In truth, however, sexual pleasure is as necessary for bodily health as food. It only becomes an obstacle to moral virtue if it is practised without restraint. Thus men and women by seeking sexual pleasure in accordance with the laws ordained by the Lord of the Universe, will in no way undermine the practice of moral virtue.

Sexual pleasure, enjoyed by a man and a woman who are married according to divine law, brings both children and respect. The husband and wife who enjoy one another in love over many decades are admired and even envied by all around them.

Harmonizing Passion

The joy of sexual intercouse consists in the man and the woman harmonizing their passion. This is partly a matter of natural capacity. There are men of small passion whose desire at the time of sexual union is tepid, whose semen is scanty, and who recoil from a woman's warm embraces. Such men should be united with women of small passion, who are also tepid, whose sexual juices are scanty and who recoil from warm embraces. There are men of middling passion, who should be united with similar women. And there are men of intense passion, whose desire burns like a fire, whose semen is plentiful, and who crave close contact with the woman's body. Such men should be united with women of intense passion.

Harmonizing passion is also a matter of artistry and

skill. The man is aroused quickly, and rises to a peak of passion, at which moment he emits his semen; then his desire is satisfied, and he wishes to discontinue coitus. The woman emits sexual juices continuously, and by this means makes coitus comfortable and smooth both for herself and for the man. She is slow to be aroused, and takes a long time to emit all her sexual juices; and only when this has occurred is she satisfied. There are two dangers. The first is that the man tries to begin full intercourse before the woman is ready, causing her pain rather than pleasure. The second is that the man reaches his peak and emits his semen too quickly, leaving the woman dissatisfied. To harmonize his passion with hers, the man must restrain his arousal, and learn to control the emission of semen until the woman is ready.

Yet such skill in harmonizing passion is useless unless there is true love between the man and the woman; only if they are bound in love will they be able to express passion in harmony. There are four kinds of love, each of which is vital for sexual fulfilment. The first is love of the eyes: the man and the woman must appreciate the beauty of each other's body. The second is love of the mind: the man and the woman must know one another's character, and respond warmly to what they know. The third is love of the imagination: the man and the woman must understand each other's desires, and be able to satisfy them. The fourth is love acquired by continual habit: if the love between the man and the woman is true, they will not grow bored by sexual activity, but its pleasure will deepen.

Embracing

There are eight kinds of embrace by which a man and a woman may indicate their sexual love.

The first two embraces are for those who as yet do not speak freely with each other, but wish to become more intimate.

i.   The Touching Embrace. The man, under some pretext or other, goes in front of or alongside the woman, and lets his body touch her body.

ii.   The Piercing Embrace. The woman bends down, as if to pick something from the ground, and pierces, as it were, the man with her breasts.

The next two embraces are especially appropriate during the early meetings of a man and a woman, indicating their hope of great joys to come.

iii. The Rubbing Embrace. The man and the woman walk slowly together, side by side, in some dark or lonely place, and allow their bodies to rub against each other.

iv.   The Pressing Embrace. One of them presses the other against a wall or a tree, and they look into each other's eyes.

The next two embraces occur when intimacy has been established. They may be engaged in themselves, or they may be a preparation for full sexual intercourse.

v.   The Twining of a Creeper. The woman, clinging to the

man as a creeper twines round the tree, puts her arms round his head and draws his mouth towards hers. She kisses him gently.

vi.   Climbing a Tree. The woman puts one foot on the man's foot and lifts the thigh of the other leg upwards so he can hold it in his hand; thus it is as if she is about to climb him. She passes one arm round his back and the other round his shoulder, and they can now kiss as they wish.

The fourth pair of embraces takes place during sexual union.

vii.   Mixing Sesame Seed and Rice. The man and the woman, lying on a bed, embrace each other so closely that the arms and thighs of one are encircled by the arms and thighs of the other.

viii.   Mixing Milk and Water. The man sits on the edge of the bed or on the floor. The woman sits on his lap, her arms round his neck and her legs round his waist.

The description of eight kinds of embrace is to be read for enjoyment, in anticipation of a loving encounter. The man and the woman who have reflected in their minds on the art of embracing will, when the opportunity comes, embrace one another with grace and elegance, as if they were gods performing a heavenly dance. But once the dance of love begins, lovers will discover for themselves numerous beautiful variations on these eight types.

Kissing

Embracing naturally leads to kissing, and kissing to sexual union. Embracing and kissing are the means whereby the fire of passion is kindled, and sexual union should not take place until the flames are beginning to rise. And embracing and kissing should continue throughout coitus, to keep the fire burning brightly. Indeed, coitus without embracing and kissing would be quite unnatural and wrong, since it would show that the man and the woman had no true love for each other, but merely wanted to satisfy their lust.

These are the places which should be kissed: the forehead, the eyes, the cheeks, the throat, the breasts, the lips, and the interior of the mouth. Some also advocate kissing the thighs, the arms and the navel, while others find such kissing offensive; it should only occur if both the man and the woman regard it as a proper expression of love.

There are four ways of kissing.

i. The Touching Kiss. The lips of the man and the woman meet, stay together without moving, and then part. If it is the first kiss, the muscles of the lips may remain hard, and the kiss last only for a moment. But if the man and the woman wish to indicate a desire for greater intimacy, the lips become soft, and the kiss is prolonged.

ii. The Breathing Kiss. The man and the woman let their mouths open, at first only slightly and then more widely, allowing the breath to mingle.

iii. The Clasping Kiss. The man opens his mouth, while the mouth of the woman remains closed, and he clasps her lips in his own. He also may force his tongue between her lips, and touch her clenched teeth. The woman may clasp the man's lips in hers; but this is only possible if the man has no moustache.

iv. The Fighting Kiss. The man and the woman open their mouths and their tongues engage in a loving battle, as each tries to explore the mouth of the other.

These are the kisses that kindle the flame of desire. Yet a man and a woman should not only kiss in anticipation of sexual union. They should give and receive kisses at many times of the day and night, to express love without seeking to kindle desire. When the woman wakes up at night, she may kiss her beloved sleeping beside her, ensuring that her touch is so gentle that he is not disturbed. When a man comes home late, he may bend over the sleeping body of his beloved, and kiss her gently on various parts. If she is only dozing, she may awaken and further intimacy may ensue; but in kindness he should never try to awaken her, to satisfy his own desire. When a man and a woman pass by a mirror together, one may kiss the reflection of the other; they may do the same when both are looking into the still waters of a lake. The smiles that follow such an expression of love give great pleasure and comfort. Most important of all, when the man and the woman have been quarrelling, they should end their quarrel with a kiss to show that all is forgiven.

There is one other kind of kiss that should be mentioned. It is not often used, but it possesses great power. One is sitting quietly, perhaps reading or engaged in some craft. The other crawls up behind, moving carefully so that there is no noise, and gently kisses their beloved's thigh or great toe. This may lead simply to a playful laugh. But it can at times instantly inflame passion, so that within seconds the fires of desire are burning.

Scratching

It may seem strange that those who love each other passionately also hurt each other in the act of loving by scratching. Yet just as the Lord of the Universe has made the world as a sign of divine love, so the marks which a man and a woman make on one another with their nails are a sign of human love. And when afterwards the man and the woman look at the marks made on their own bodies, their love is renewed and rekindled.

There are eight kinds of scratching or pressing with the nails.

i.   Sounding. The skin is pressed with the nail so lightly that no mark is made. The nail is pulled across the skin gently so that the hairs are pushed up, and a soft noise is made. This is especially pleasurable if the man and the woman are bathing together. One may apply shampoo to the other's body and then gently pull a nail across the soapy skin.

34

ii. New Moon. A mark is made by pressing a single nail into the skin. And since a nail is slightly curved, the mark looks like a new moon.

iii. Circle. A circular mark is made, round the navel or on the buttocks.

iv. Line. A straight line is scratched, usually on the back. This is often done at the height of passion, when the pain of the scratch becomes an exquisite pleasure.

v. Tiger's Tail. A curved line is scratched on the back, again at the height of passion.

vi. Peacock's Foot. A curved mark is made on the breast, usually with all five nails of a hand. This requires great skill.

vii. Jump of a Hare. The marks of the five nails are close, around the nipple of a breast.

viii. Leaf of a Lotus. A mark is made on the breast or the hips, in the shape of a blue lotus leaf.

Those with imagination may think of other marks that can be made, for marking the body of one's lover is truly a work of art. It can be especially important when the man or the woman is about to go away on a journey: a mark made by nails on some hidden part of the body is a special token of remembrance.

Biting

The passion of love and the passion of anger are closely related. The Lord of the Universe has ordered that the act of love is, as it were, also a battle between the man and the woman. In love each tries to give pleasure to the other; in battle each seeks to seize as much pleasure. Thus for the pleasure of sexual union to be fully enjoyed, an element of anger must be expressed. And the best means of expressing anger is through biting.

Yet man and woman must be aware that biting carries dangers. When they scratch each other, they may cause pain, but can do little harm, because the fingers are not sufficiently strong. But even a woman's jaw has power to draw blood and cause serious injury. So when the man and woman bite one another, they must be sure to hold back their full strength.

There are eight different kinds of biting.

i.   The Hidden Bite. The bite is gentle so the teeth leave no imprint. But it lasts sufficiently long to make the skin red.

ii. The Swollen Bite. The skin is pressed down on both sides, causing it to swell in the middle.

iii. The Line of Points. A series of small bites is inflicted in a straight line across the skin.

iv. Coral and Jewel. The bite is made between the upper teeth – the jewel – and the lower lip – the coral.

v.   Line of Jewels. This can only be done on a soft part of the anatomy such as the buttocks or, in the case of a fat person, the stomach. The person giving the bite takes as much of the other person's flesh into their mouth as they can manage, and bites with all their teeth.

vi.   Cumulus Cloud. This can be done gently on the woman's breasts. A series of coral and jewel bites is made across the breast, to give a shape of clouds.

vii. Tiger's Mauling. At the height of passion, when the man and the woman are in full sexual union, they can most easily bite one another's shoulders. Like a tiger mauling an animal, they will make random marks.

viii. Gnarled Tree Stump. When the man or the woman are about to go away on a journey, they may wish to leave marks on one another with their teeth. By ancient custom the thigh is where such marks are made. A series of marks are made up and down the thigh, so that the skin looks like the bark of an old tree.

Striking

Throughout all ages husbands and wives have quarrelled; and usually the more trivial the matter, the fiercer has been the argument. During these quarrels husbands and wives sometimes exchange blows, not in order to injure one another, but as an expression of emotion. Those who wish to enjoy true sexual fulfilment must realize that in all respects, quarrels included, sexual activity should mirror life itself. So it is natural that from time to time the man and the woman should exchange blows. And, to add to the pleasure, the one receiving the blow should let out a sound.

There are four kinds of striking.

i. Striking with the back of the hand. This can be done between the breasts.

ii. Striking with the front of the hand, the top of the fingers bent forwards. This is best done on the hips.

iii. Striking with the clenched fist. This should be done only on the back.

iv. Striking with the open palm of the hand. This suits the buttocks.

Like biting, striking can be dangerous. In particular a strong man can break the bones of a small, slightly-built woman. So a man, far from using his full force, should strike carefully. The woman, who by nature is weaker, can show less restraint.

There are four kinds of sounds which the person receiving the blows may utter.

i. A high-pitched cry.

ii. A low-pitched groan.

iii. A prolonged wail.

iv. A coo of painful pleasure.

Uniting

The various positions in which the man and the woman can unite their sexual organs can be discovered by looking at the different kinds of animals and birds. Each species has its own manner of coitus and we can seek to imitate them. But there are few people with the patience to make such observations. So the great sages, having themselves studied animals and birds, can enumerate the positions. There are four basic positions.

i.   Yawning Position. The woman lies on her back and opens her legs. The man may kneel between her legs, lift her buttocks and enter her; or he may lie on top of her and enter.

ii. Mounting Position. The woman either lies face downwards, resting on her stomach and breasts, or kneels and bends forward, supporting herself on her hands. The man enters from behind.

iii. Crab's Position. The man and the woman lie side by side, facing each other. He should be on his left, and she on her right. She lifts her left thigh, perhaps resting it on his hip. He moves forward to enter her. They may clasp one another's bodies as their nipples touch, or they may lie back; the latter manner allows extra strength for movement.

iv. Supported Position. The woman leans against a wall or a pillar. She may remain standing, or the man may hold her thighs in his hands. If he is strong he can put his hands together to make a seat for her; and in the passion of love she can push herself away from the wall and cling onto his neck, so he is supporting her whole weight.

In addition to these basic positions, people in different parts of the country use a number of variations.

i.   Crab's Position. Lying on her back, the woman pulls her knees up towards her breasts, so her yoni is raised up.

ii.   Rising Position. Lying on her back, the woman raises both her legs straight upwards. She may place them on the man's shoulders.

iii. Lotus Position – for the woman. The woman crosses her legs and lies back.

iv.   Lotus Position – for the man. The man crosses his legs, so the lingam points straight upwards. The woman sits on his lap.

v.   Clasping Position. After the man has entered, the woman closes her legs, clasping his lingam inside.

vi.   Squeezing Position. The woman puts her thighs round his waist and squeezes.

vii. Mare's Position. Using the strength within her yoni, the woman presses on his lingam. She may give extra pleasure by pressing for a few moments, then relaxing – and repeating this a number of times. This technique requires practice for women, but it is said that mares can do it naturally.

viii.   Elephant's Position. The man and the woman stand up in water and unite, as elephants do.

In all these positions the woman is offering herself to the man, and he plays the active part. But there are times when any man is too tired to be active, and yet the woman is filled with desire. This may occur in the middle of coitus: the man through exhaustion wishes to conclude, but the woman is not yet satisfied. Or it may occur from the start: the man is too tired to initiate coitus, but the woman is keen. In these circumstances the woman should play the part of the man. He should lie back on the bed. She may lie on him, their breasts touching. She may sit on him, either facing him or looking at his feet. Then she may lift his back against a wall and crouch on his lap. All this will give both pleasure and rest to the man, and the woman will satisfy herself.

Moving

When the lingam is in the yoni, there are nine movements that the man may make, and three movements that the woman may make. These are the man's movements.

i.   Moving Forward. The lingam moves slowly and gently into the yoni, penetrating her deeply.
ii.   Churning. The man holds the lingam and moves it round the yoni.
iii.   Piercing. The man lifts himself so that the lingam presses against the upper part of the yoni. This is

where the tongue of the yoni is situated, so this movement gives the woman the greatest pleasure.

iv. Rubbing. The man lifts the woman's buttocks, perhaps placing a cushion beneath them, so that the lingam presses against the lower part of the yoni. This is very restful for the woman.

v. Pressing. The lingam remains pressed deep inside the yoni, without moving.

vi. Striking. The lingam is lodged just inside the yoni; then suddenly the lingam is thrust forward.

vii. Blow of a Boar. The lingam is pushed against only one side of the yoni.

viii. Blow of a Bull. As the lingam is moved forward and back, it is also moved from side to side.

ix. Sparrow's Jerks. The lingam is moved very fast. This should be done as the climax is being reached.

The woman's movements are these.

i. Pair of Tongs. The woman holds the lingam in her yoni, drawing it in and out, and pressing it.

ii. Turning. With the man lying on his back, the woman sits on him and turns from side to side. The agile woman may even turn full circles with the lingam in her yoni.

iii. Swinging. The man lifts himself up so that only his shoulders and feet are on the ground. The woman sits astride him and swings forward and back. If the man is not sufficiently strong, he may place cushions under his back.

Mouth Intercourse

There are special pleasures to be gained if the woman lets her mouth play the part of her yoni. Some regard this as unnatural. But since every pleasure that men and women enjoy together strengthens their mutual love, mouth congress is to be regarded as a gift bestowed by the Lord of the Universe.

There are six favours which a woman may do with her mouth to the lingam.

i.   Sucking a Mango Fruit. She puts half in her mouth, and sucks it as if she were extracting juice from a mango fruit.

ii.   Biting a Banana. She puts half in her mouth and bites it, with the same force with which one would bite a soft banana.

iii.   Blowing a Flute. She imagines the lingam is a flute. She takes it into her mouth and closes her lips over it. Then she blows, opening her lips slightly to release the air. And she strokes the end with her tongue, as if making a note.

iv.   Eating Sugar Cane. She takes the whole lingam into her mouth and sucks, moving her mouth up and down, as if taking the sweetness out of a stick of sugar cane. She may allow her teeth to touch the lingam as she moves, as if she were pulling the sweetness from the cane's rough fibres.

v.   Licking a Melon. Just as one may lick a melon to enjoy the sweet taste, moving the tongue all over it, she may lick the lingam, moving her tongue up, down and round.

vi. Swallowing a Fish. Just as sea-birds swallow whole fish in their beaks, she may take the whole lingam deeply into her mouth and begin to swallow. Care should be taken that she does not choke. This may cause the man pain, but this itself will add to the pleasure.

A man may honour his wife by kissing her yoni. And when the fire of her passion is burning brightly he may do to the tongue of her yoni the things that she may do with her mouth to the lingam. Those men and women who are slim and agile may give pleasure to one another simultaneously, lying in the inverted position, with the man kissing her yoni and the woman sucking his lingam. This is known as 'the union of a crow'.

Beginning and Ending

Sexual intercourse may give pleasure, but will give no satisfaction if the circumstances are dull and drab. The reason is that, while lust can be stimulated by the proximity of two bodies, the true passion of love can never flourish amidst ugliness. Love between a man and a woman should be reflected in the elegance of the room in which they meet, in the fragrance of her perfume and of the flowers around the bed, and even in the distant sound of music or of bells. In such surroundings crude lust is elevated to divine love. And as the man and the woman embrace, kiss, touch and then unite, they will be like a god and goddess meeting in heaven.

When sexual union is complete the man and the woman should not separate, each rushing to perform some new task or enjoy some fresh pleasure. They should linger for many minutes in each other's arms, enjoying the sensation of the warm moisture of their skin mingling. He may then rise and apply some sweet-smelling ointment to her reclining body. Then they may sit quietly together, eating sweetmeats and drinking fresh juice of the mango fruit. Finally she may rest her head in his lap, and they may share that special kind of conversation which sounds like nonsense to an eavesdropper but is filled with meaning for those who love one another.

ANANGA-RANGA

The author of this twelfth-century sex manual, Kalyana Malla, condemns any kind of sexual activity outside marriage, stating that his purpose is to enable couples to remain faithful. And since sexual boredom is the main danger to fidelity, couples must therefore learn variety and excitement in their lovemaking. Much of the book repeats the instructions of the *Kama Sutra*. But he devotes special attention to the varying sexual needs of different types of women. And he is particularly concerned with the sexual and emotional problems that undermine marriage.

Playing a Woman

This work is dedicated to you, God of Love, who give joy, pleasure and energy to the world. It is offered to those who wish to study the art and the mystery of mankind's highest earthly delight, and who wish to practise the art. The sages of old have rightly said that our greatest satisfaction comes from contemplating the Divine Creator, the Lord of the Universe, and in this way we prepare ourselves for future lives. In the present life, however, there is no greater happiness than that derived from the love of a woman.

But sadly many men fail to enjoy this love to the full, and even become indifferent to the woman's charms. The reason is that they remain ignorant of the true needs and feelings of the woman, and simply try to satisfy their own animal lust. In this way not only do they come to despise the woman, but their own potency diminishes and even dies. Such men are themselves no better than the lowliest of animals, and should be regarded with the same contempt as they have for women.

Men who wish to enjoy the sublime delights of love must study the needs and passions of women. Then they must learn to play a woman as a musician plays his instrument. The musician regards his instrument not merely as some inert material thing, but as a creature of great delicacy, charm and feeling; and he acquires with great care and diligence the skills required to produce a beautiful sound, adapting his own movements to the instrument's needs. A man must look upon his woman with even greater respect, and with great care and diligence must learn the act of satisfying her, adapting his own movements to her needs. In this way, just as the musician is entranced by the sound of his own playing, so the man will be overjoyed by his own loving artistry. It has often been said that the sweet harmony of music reflects the divine harmony of the heavens. The harmony that can be attained between a man and a woman is heaven itself.

Classes of Women

The man who wishes to understand the female of our species must recognize that there are four types of women, who each have different needs.

Firstly there is the lotus woman. Her face and body are well covered with flesh. Her complexion is soft and yet highly-coloured, like a cloud about to burst. Her eyes are bright and seem to sparkle, like drops of rain sparkling in the sunlight. Her bosoms are firm, full and high. Her neck is round, with no signs of bone or sinew showing through the flesh. And her stomach is spongy, with three folds. When she walks, she waddles like a duck on land, and her voice is low and musical. Despite her ample flesh she eats little and sleeps lightly. She is intelligent and courteous.

Secondly there is the whimsy woman. She is slim and agile. Her limbs are strong and lean, and can spring into action rapidly. Her eyes are often motionless, as if she were staring at her prey, but when she is excited they dart from side to side. Her gait is nimble and elegant. Her complexion is usually fair, but when passion rises it fills with colour. She works hard, and she plays hard, enjoying every pleasure to the full. She has a high voice and sings sweetly. She is witty and sharp, and if roused to anger is rude and cruel.

Thirdly there is the chauk-shell woman. At most times she moves slowly in both mind and body, and she can even seem dull and foolish. But she possesses great charm, and when she wishes can outpace everyone in the speed of her thoughts and the agility of her body. Her complexion shines, and seems to change colour with the times of the day: when the sun is high she is fair, even pale, and when the sun is low she becomes dark. She delights in wearing brightly-coloured clothes, and in having flowers in her hair. Usually she is gentle, but she can suddenly become violently angry, shouting out words which poison the ears of those who hear.

Fourthly there is the elephant woman. She is stout, and always moves slowly and deliberately. She is never angry, and her word can always be trusted. She has large, moist lips, and a warm, full smile. Her skin can be rough, and her complexion red. Her neck bulges a little, her breasts are large and soft, and her belly ample, as if she had a pillow beneath her dress. She enjoys food, and eats large amounts. She sleeps heavily, and remains in bed for many hours. She is always kind and generous, with a pleasant word for everyone.

After careful study most women are found to fit approximately into one of these categories. Some have elements from two categories. A few contain elements from three or even all four categories. Only when a man has discovered which class of woman he loves can be begin to satisfy her.

Satisfying the Woman

Each type of woman has different needs. These can be specified very precisely.

The lotus woman does not want coitus at night. Her passions rise with the rising sun, and decline with the setting sun. So the man may come to her in the morning if he wants fresh, eager passion, yet with little energy; he may come at midday if he desires energetic, forceful love; and he may come in the evening if he wants slow, languid love. Her neck is especially sensitive, so when he is embracing her he should ensure that he bathes her neck in kisses. As her passion increases she begins to stroke her body, and he should also stroke her, moving his hand up and down her hips and thighs. When he has entered her, he should not move jerkily, nor make sudden changes in his rhythm; she enjoys a steady rhythm within her, with gradual changes from one type of thrust to another. Of the four basic positions of coitus, the one she enjoys most is when she is lying on her back and the man is on top.

The whimsy woman wants coitus only at night. During the day her energies are absorbed in domestic business, and only at night will she surrender herself to passion. When the man begins to embrace and kiss her, the passion within her quickly rises, and she may even want him to enter her before he is ready. During coitus she scratches and bites the man freely, often growling as she does so; and she enjoys being bitten and scratched herself, letting out cries and yelps. Her climax is wild and forceful, but when it is over she lies back motionless and exhausted, all her strength spent. Of the basic positions of coitus, the one she enjoys most is when she and the man are standing up. This allows her to move more freely and to twine her legs round the man's calves and thighs.

The chauk-shell woman enjoys variety in the time and the style of coitus. Early in the morning, as she begins to feel the heat of the sun, she enjoys strong, passionate love, which reaches its climax rapidly. In the afternoon, when the sun's heat is at its height and her body is moist with sweat, she enjoys long, slow love, with much time spent kissing and embracing prior to full union; it may take an hour or even longer to reach a climax, in which the body's movements remain calm but the inner joy is intense. In the evening, as the dark air cools, she enjoys bringing herself and the man to the brink of climax, and then lying about motionless while passions subside; and she repeats the pattern a number of times before the climax is finally attained. She rarely moves fast during coitus, but her body slithers and writhes as passion rises, and at the climax she often opens her mouth wide and bites the man's neck, pressing her tongue against the flesh clasped between her teeth. Of the basic positions, the one she enjoys most is lying side by side, allowing her to slither and writhe freely on the bed.

The elephant woman has so much flesh that she is hardly aware of the changing temperature. So she can enjoy coitus equally at any time. She always welcomes the man's embraces and kisses, but it takes a long time to arouse her passion sufficiently for coitus to begin. She neither bites nor scratches, and her movements are always slow; but when passion is in full flood the flesh on her body and thighs trembles. She is happy for the man to change the rhythm and force of his thrust as he wishes, while she passively receives his love. Of the four basic positions the one she enjoys most is lying face downwards, her body resting on her ample bosoms and stomach, while the man mounts her from above. In this way she can relax completely while receiving pleasure from the man.

A woman cannot change her nature, and must love according to her nature. A man, by contrast, is more flexible. He plays the active part, and must adapt his own style of love according to the woman's nature. If he ignores her needs, she will feel unloved and so be unable to respond to him; in this way neither of them will be satisfied. But if he understands which type of woman he possesses, and acts accordingly, both will enjoy such intense joy that they will never want to separate.

Overcoming Problems

Sadly good marriages sometimes go wrong, and the love which a woman once had for her husband fades to indifference, which may even turn to hatred. There are various signs of such indifference. In conversation the woman no longer looks the man in the eyes. If he asks her a question, she is reluctant to reply. When the man draws near to her, her face remains impassive, and she may even back away. At night when he indicates desire, she says she is too tired and ready for sleep. When he kisses her, she jerks her face away. She regards his friends with contempt, enjoying malicious gossip about them, and she treats his family with disrespect. When a man notices these signs he may feel helpless to win back her love. But he must look for the causes of her indifference, and then take action to overcome them.

There are twelve reasons why a woman may turn away from her husband, each of which can be overcome.

i.   She remains under the influence of her mother, who resents the rights which her husband now has over her, and tries to undermine him in her daughter's eyes. In such a case he must be ruthless in preventing any contact between mother and daughter.

ii.   Her friends are depraved, lacking any moral sense, and indulging in lewd and malicious talk. Again he must be ruthless in breaking such relationships.

iii.   The husband spends excessive time away from her, either on business or in pursuit of pleasure. Such a husband forfeits his conjugal rights; and if he wishes to regain them, he must commit himself anew to his wife.

iv.   The husband gives her too little money for clothes, or he fails to notice the trouble she takes over her appearance. A woman whose beauty is ignored by her husband naturally turns to other men for compliments. So the husband must learn to appreciate her beauty for himself.

v.   The husband is too proud and haughty to listen to his wife's views on both domestic and worldly affairs. A wife whose intelligence is not valued becomes bored and melancholic, and loses her appetite for love.

vi.   The husband uses rough and filthy language in his wife's presence. His wife naturally concludes that a man who shows so little care with his words is also careless in love. He must learn good manners in words and in love.

vii. The husband shows undue interest in other women, even speaking highly of them to his wife. At first she will react with jealousy. But eventually jealousy turns to hatred and she hardens her heart to her husband's infidelity.

viii. The husband is violent and cruel, even hitting his wife when he feels angry or frustrated. It is a matter of deep alarm that such men are common, and even more shameful that they expect their wives to rise from the ground and have coitus with them. The joyful harmony of coitus depends on the husband and wife speaking and acting harmoniously throughout their life together.

ix.   The husband is constantly suspicious of his wife, and demands to know everything she has done or said. A wife who is truly trusted by her husband becomes trustworthy; a wife who is not trusted cannot help but yearn for other men.

x.   The husband becomes sexually impotent and so fails to satisfy his wife. Impotence usually stems from selfishness: the man is so anxious about himself and his capacity for pleasure that this anxiety may destroy that capacity. Thus he must look within his own heart, and through meditation turn his heart from himself to his wife. Once she feels loved by him, she will enable him to rediscover his potency. While he concentrates on her beauty, seeking to please her with kisses and caresses, she can gently stir his lingam back to life.

xi.   The husband does not bathe sufficiently often, nor

wash his clothes, so that he smells and looks dirty. Though his wife may love him from afar, once he comes near she will find herself unable to respond.

xii. Coitus is dull and monotonous, following the same pattern on each occasion. The husband must study and practise the numerous different positions for coitus, the different ways of kissing and embracing, and the different methods of thrusting. The four classes of women each have preferences, so the husband should give special emphasis to these. But all women like variety, and it is this which can keep their passion alive for ten, twenty, thirty, forty or even fifty years.

BUDDHISM

INTRODUCTION: BUDDHISM

Buddhism, which grew out of Hinduism, followed the ascetic, rather than the sensual, tradition of Indian religion; and as a result it was initially hostile to sexual pleasure. Yet as it spread northwards into Tibet, China and Japan it gradually acquired a more positive attitude.

Gautama, who became the Buddha, was a minor Indian prince, and as a young man married a beautiful princess and lived in a palace. But he felt increasingly dissatisfied with his comfortable life, and oppressed by the misery he saw around him. So one night at the age of twenty-nine he slipped out of his palace and adopted the life of a wandering monk. At first he imposed a most rigid discipline on himself, denying himself all food and sleep until he was little more than a skeleton. Eventually he found peace in the 'Middle Way' between pleasure and austerity, in which food and rest could be enjoyed in moderation, but sexual pleasure remained forbidden.

A community of monks soon formed round the Buddha, and this became the model for the monasteries which continue to flourish. He taught that sexual desire upsets the soul's inner calm, so he urged his monks not even to speak to a woman until they had completely overcome their sexual instinct. Later monastic rules also forbid masturbation, although they recognize that monks have no control over their dreams, and thus should not be ashamed of ejaculating in their sleep.

To this day Buddhism in southeast Asia remains largely negative towards physical sensuality. But quite different, more flamboyant forms of Buddhism developed in the Himalayan mountains and in northeast Asia. In Tibet a distinction was drawn between right-hand and left-hand religious principles. Right-hand principles assert that only in total emptiness could truth be found; thus the individual must detach himself from all material pleasures and desires, and exist in a spiritual void. Left-hand principles assert that truth must be discovered through the pursuit of pleasure, including sexual pleasure, and the individual should learn how to enhance his capacity for pleasure to its utmost limit. To the logical mind these two sets of principles seem contradictory, but to Tibetan philosophers they offered alternative, and equally valid, paths to enlightenment. Sadly few texts on sexual themes survive, but we do possess one remarkable extract from a large thesis, describing how middle-aged couples can revive their sexual potency and thus continue their pursuit of pleasure.

It is, however, the Zen Buddhism of Japan that offers the greatest insights. It sought to reconcile the principles of detachment and pleasure, and did this by making a sharp distinction between desire and pleasure. The disciple of the Buddha should free himself of all physical desire, including sexual desire, and thus become detached from the world; this detachment will bring inner peace and contentment. Yet the absence of desire does not eliminate the capacity for pleasure, but rather increases it. Thus the person with no sexual desire can actually enjoy sexual intercourse as a wonderful gift. In particular the violent feelings which can mar sexual activity are absent, so intercourse is a true celebration of spiritual harmony. This harmony is symbolized in the Zen Circle of Love in which a man and a woman, sitting face to face with their legs around each other's torsos and the sexual parts in union, form their bodies into a perfect circle.

TSOGYEL

Married to the Emperor of Tibet at the age of thirteen, he in turn presented her three years later to a Buddhist monastery, to serve at table. The abbot, however, took advantage of her, forcing her to be his mistress. After his death she became a religious teacher in her own right, and also took a new husband. She sought to reconcile the Buddha's emphasis on celibacy with sexual pleasure by teaching that people should only engage in sexual activity if they had control of their desires. In this way sexual pleasure can be enjoyed as a divine gift, without disturbing the soul's inner peace.

Sexual Philosophy

Medicine and poison have opposite effects on the body, yet in essence they are the same. In the same way sexual activity and sexual abstinence are opposites, yet in essence they should be the same. The person who follows the way of abstinence seeks to purge the body of all sexual desire, and in this way experiences the divine bliss of celibacy. Similarly the person who is sexually active will only experience the true divinely-ordered pleasure of coitus if there is no lustful desire.

The person who is filled with sexual desire can never be satisfied. Lust is a form of aggression in which the individual seeks to possess a sexual partner for bodily gratification. And the sexual act arising from lust is often violent, the man and the woman each trying to seize pleasure for themselves. If the man ejaculates he enjoys momentary fulfilment, but he soon becomes restless and discontented, waiting for his potency to return so he can indulge himself again. And if he does not ejaculate his entire body remains agitated, and he seethes with frustration. Similarly the woman driven by desire wants far more sexual activity than her lustful man is able to give, and an orgasm brings only temporary relief. In short, desire always outstrips pleasure, so the body remains unfulfilled.

The pleasure of coitus is a gift, to be received with gratitude. The mind should not dwell on it, nor the body lust after it. The person who is sexually active should aspire to the same inner peacefulness as the hermit in a remote cave. Thus when it is appropriate to share sexual pleasure with another person it brings unalloyed joy. And when that time together is complete, the man and the woman are as peaceful as before.

Sexual activity between a man and a woman free of desire has no aggression. The man sees himself as the medium through which the gift of pleasure is bestowed on the woman; and the woman sees herself as the means of pleasure for the man. Thus the mind of each is focused on the pleasure of the other. In this way there is a true and complete mingling of the man's white seed and the woman's red seed, to form a divine nectar. At the end of coitus the man and the woman absorb this nectar into their bodies, and enjoy a most wonderful peace – the peace which the Buddha has called 'pleasure beyond pleasure'.

Transformation of Desire

Men and women who have sought freedom from desire have often gone to remote caves, and lived alone for many years, meditating day and night. Yet frequently their efforts are fruitless. Worse still, sexual desire is magnified. The woman's meditations are filled with thoughts of young naked men kissing and fondling her breasts and presenting their members to her yoni. And the man's meditations are filled with thoughts of young naked women offering their bodies to him. Thus the lonely cave in which these insatiable dreams occur becomes a living hell.

The reason for this misery is that such people try to destroy desire. This is impossible. Desire can never be removed or repressed by the human will. If a person wishes to break free from slavery, then desire must be transformed, so that the individual becomes the master, not the slave.

This transformation takes place at three levels. Firstly the level of the body. The person who is the slave of physical desire finds that the body becomes sexually agitated at any time. Without warning the man's lingam becomes erect and the woman's yoni moist, and the entire body is agitated. The man who seeks freedom learns to determine the time of erection, as he is master of his own lingam. And the woman becomes mistress of her yoni by determining the times when it becomes moist. Thus when sexual activity is appropriate, they are ready for it; and when it is inappropriate, their bodies are at rest. To achieve such control requires the wisdom to recognize the body's own natural rhythm. Each body has a certain degree of sexual energy, a young person's more than an older person's; and this energy must be released. The person who has control over the body is able to choose the moment of release.

Secondly the level of the mind. The way of enlightenment taught by the Buddha requires the individual to control all thoughts. Sexual thoughts only cause misery when they swill helplessly round the brain, like filthy water in a sewer. But when sexual activity is appropriate, the person with control over the mind can bring into the brain the most sweet, enchanting thoughts which can turn mere physical pleasure into the most intense mental ecstasy.

Thirdly the level of the spirit. The Buddha teaches that nirvana is the union of the individual spirit with the universal spirit. The person with control over the spirit experiences sexual activity as a fragment of nirvana. Through the bodily and mental union of the man and the woman, their spirits are also unified. This occurs when the man seeks nothing for himself, but is absorbed wholly in the woman's joy; and the woman seeks nothing for herself, but is absorbed wholly in the man's joy.

The transformation of desire is not easy, and is achieved only in small steps, over many months and years. Yet as the individual gets nearer the goal a strange discovery is made: the bliss from sexual activity is ever greater, but the need for sexual activity is ever smaller. The person who has complete control is the most perfect lover, who gives and receives perfect joy. Yet that same person is happy to be alone in a remote cave, without any sexual contact. That is the example of the Buddha, who was the perfect lover, yet chose to be celibate.

GHANTAPA

A Buddhist monk in ancient India, he at first practised the most rigid self-discipline, including celibacy; and he frequently accused the king of debauchery. The king retaliated by sending a beautiful young woman to live near him, and eventually the monk was overwhelmed with desire. The king now accused the monk of debauchery, who replied by humbly apologizing for his earlier self-righteousness. The monk and the young woman married, and he became a famous teacher on sexual matters. His particular concern was to help men who had become impotent to revive their sexual powers.

The Laws of Love

To the God of Love, the friend of the world, the source of the greatest joy, be praise and glory! When he rises in the heart of a man or a woman, he overcomes all resistance. The bees are his servants, the birds are his poets, the moon is his eye, the soft breeze from the sea his breath. The slender woman is his bow, sidelong glances are his quiver, kisses are his arrows.

The pleasures of the world are like water in a basket; they drain away as quickly as they are poured in. So if we are to enjoy life, the stock of pleasure must constantly be replenished. The man and the woman who study carefully the laws of the God of Love, and follow them diligently, will find that the joy of love is unending. Desire for one another is renewed daily, and potency restored. Those who fail to study and follow those laws, by contrast, soon find that the joy of love goes stale, and potency dwindles.

Some older men and women despair of ever regaining desire and potency. In their youth they failed to follow love's laws, and now suffer for it. Yet it is never too late to learn. Even in the fifties, sixties or seventies men and women can begin to study those laws, and gradually their desire and potency will return. Such is the God of Love's great mercy!

There is a further reason to study the laws of love. There are many people who are married in name, but whose hearts are far apart. Perhaps in their youth they loved and enjoyed one another. But now they are cool and indifferent, finding no joy in each other. The husband may find that he is no longer capable of an erection; and the woman's yoni may be permanently dry and arid, like desert sand.

For all those who feel little or no desire, whose potency has diminished, whose hearts are cold, the God of Love has revealed through the stars fourteen steps to the renewal of love. It is important that the first step is taken when the moon is new. Then each night a further step is taken. By the time the moon is full, desire and potency will be restored.

Fourteen Steps of Love

On the first night, when the moon is new, the man begins by kissing the woman's forehead, moving down to her cheeks. He strokes her head and ruffles up her hair. As she responds, he moves his lips to her lips. They kiss with their lips closed, but after a while he opens his lips slightly, wraps his lips over her teeth, and presses her lips between his. He does not attempt to undress her, but at times strokes her back. If the flames of desire begin to rise, they stop kissing and caressing until the flames are subdued. Their only purpose on this first day is to relax together.

On the second night, they again start very slowly, doing all the things they did on the first day. But when he opens his mouth, he presses his tongue between her lips to encourage her to open her mouth. Thus they allow their breath to mingle. After stroking her back, he lets his hand fall to her buttocks and thighs.

On the third night they relax together as on the previous days. But now the particular focus of his attention is her breasts. As she warms to his embraces he moves his hand to her bosoms and begins to fondle them. Then he stoops down and kisses them. Still he does not undress her, so the sensation she feels is very slight. They continue to avoid excitement; their purpose is gently and cautiously to rediscover each other's bodies.

On the fourth night they begin to fan the flame of passion, but remaining careful to avoid the blaze of desire. When they kiss he presses his tongue between her lips;

and as she opens her lips, he pushes his tongue into her mouth until their tongues meet. They now engage in a pleasurable battle. As the battle proceeds they will want to press their bodies together, as if intercourse was about to begin. But as soon as that desire overwhelms them, the battle should cease, and they should resume their gentle caresses.

On the fifth night they repeat the actions of the fourth day. But now, as passion rises, they do press their bodies together. They are still dressed, so no greater intimacy can occur. Yet they can thrust their pelvises forward and back, as if they were engaged in a dance.

On the sixth and seventh night they do again what they did on the fifth day. The man who had thought himself impotent, and the woman who had been dry, will now find that the lingam rises and the yoni becomes moist. But on no account should either the man or the woman reach a climax, as this would dissipate their desire. The purpose of this stage is to build and sustain desire.

On the eighth night the man and the woman undress down to their waists. As they kiss and caress the man loosens the woman's bodice, and lets it fall to the floor. He presses her naked bosoms against his naked chest, but does not touch her bosoms with his hands or his lips.

On the ninth night they again undress down to their waists. The man touches the underside of the woman's breasts. If she is not sufficiently stimulated she may brush his hand away. But once the flames of passion are rising she will welcome his touch. He caresses the top and bottom of her breasts gently, and then with great delicacy touches her nipples. Then with equal delicacy he kisses her nipples.

On the tenth night the man and the woman undress completely. Even if they have been married for many years and decades, this moment will bring much excitement, as if they were seeing each other's bodies for the first time. During the previous nine days their desire for each other will have grown, and now, as he looks at her yoni and she at his lingam, the thought of consummating that desire will fill their minds. But on this occasion they must not touch each other's sexual parts. And they should not let passion become so intense that they reach a climax; if there is a danger of this they should both dress.

On the eleventh night they again undress, and then cover each other with kisses from head to toe. But they should carefully avoid kissing each other's sexual parts, even though the temptation to do so will be intensely strong.

On the twelfth night they again cover each other with kisses. The man sucks the woman's nipples, at first very gently and then with more vigour, until she is panting with excitement. The woman kisses all round the lingam, licking the upper part of his thigh and his scrotum, but not touching the lingam itself; he too will pant with excitement.

On the thirteenth night, having kissed and caressed every other part of each other's bodies, they let their lips touch each other's sexual parts. He kisses her yoni, and with his tongue strokes the yoni's tongue. She kisses the lingam, stroking it from the base to the tip with her tongue. The urge to reach a climax will be intense, but they must resist. If he feels he is about to ejaculate he must ask her to desist.

By the fourteenth night the moon is full, and so is their love. If the lingam was flaccid and the yoni dry at the new moon, now the lingam is firm and strong, and the yoni flows with the juices of love. The man feels confident and relaxed, his old fears having melted away in the heat of desire. The woman, who once felt indifferent to the man's body, now regards it as divinely beautiful. So it is time for the lingam to enter the yoni. This should not be done quickly or forcefully, or else he will reach a climax almost at once, leaving her unsatisfied. Rather much time should be spent kissing and caressing, to fan the flames of passion, yet not allowing the heat to become too fierce. Once the fire is burning steadily, he should enter her, slowly slipping the lingam into her yoni until it is deep inside; there he should rest motionless for a few moments. Let them absorb the joy of this achievement, giving thanks to the God of Love who has made it possible. Now he can begin thrusting, at first gently and then more rapidly until the climax is reached.

These fourteen steps, from the new moon to the full moon, can renew desire and potency even in couples who have become utterly indifferent to one another. But once potency is restored, they must beware of letting it dwindle again. They must study the teachings of the sages on all the different styles of coitus, so that constant variety keeps the flame of passion burning.

IKKYU

The son of the Japanese emperor by one of the royal concubines, he was sent at the age of five to be educated in a Zen monastery. As a young adult he left in disgust, after discovering that many of the monks had illicit sexual liaisons, while pretending to be celibate. He came to believe that the 'red thread of passion' cannot be broken, but must be integrated into the religious life. He first described the famous Zen Circle in which a man and a woman in sexual union symbolize divine harmony.

The Zen Circle

A gentle breeze blows over the lotus pond, and stirs the man and the woman who are resting under a tree near the bank. They rise up and sit facing one another on the prayer mat. They put their thighs round each other's hips, and he slips his Zen tool into her lotus boat. 'My body is yours, and your body is mine,' each says to the other. Together they form a perfect, unbroken circle.

The Red Thread

To follow the way of enlightenment, there is an essential point that you must understand and accept: the red thread of passion between our legs cannot be severed. Some believe they can sever it, and spend many years mortifying the flesh; but their efforts prove fruitless.

Equally to follow the way of enlightenment that red thread of passion must not be allowed to entangle the entire body and soul. Some believe that they can indulge every desire without restraint, and give way to every passion without skill or artistry. Yet they will find that bodily pleasure will soon diminish, and that their souls will remain agitated and unhappy.

If understood aright, the red thread of passion can be woven into a warm seamless garment which can provide warmth and comfort. A man and a woman whose souls and bodies are in union, and who have learnt to practise sexual love with restraint and with artistry, will be far happier as they follow the path of the Buddha.

An Abbot's Disgust

I was asked to be abbot of an illustrious monastery. I was told that the monks were celibate, devoting their time to meditation and the study of sacred texts; yet any woman who came to see them in search of wise counsel was seduced. I was told that the monks lived in peace and harmony; but they constantly squabbled over who should have the most beautiful women and the tastiest food. So I left, and cleansed my soul of such hypocrisy by spending a week in a brothel, and a further week imbibing strong liquor.

Wise Folly

If you follow the rule of celibacy blindly, you are no more than an ass. If you break it, you are only human. Better to be a fallible human than a blind ass. But be fallible wisely, with a good and faithful woman.

Cure for Impotence

I wanted to devote myself to sexual passion. I wanted the red thread of passion to entangle me from head to foot. But after ten years of pleasure with many different women, my jade stalk withered. I was still crazy with desire, but was incapable of satisfaction.

Then a blind minstrel came to see me. She had never seen herself in the mirror, so she did not know how beautiful she was. Nor could she see that I was now an old man, wrinkled with age. At the very sight of her my jade stalk sprouted. And as we talked I realized that my jade stalk had foretold my emotions; my heart swelled with love for her. She was slower and more cautious, but at last she fell in love with me.

Now we live together in perfect harmony. At night she sings to me, and then our bodies unite, forming a perfect circle of love. Since our hearts are in union, and since I know she will always be faithful to me, my jade stalk will sprout whenever we come together in love.

Many people who knew I was impotent, and who suffer the same distress themselves, come to me for advice. 'How was your impotence cured?' they ask; 'and can we be cured in the same way?' My reply is simple. 'When I wanted a different woman every night, and cared nothing for love and faithfulness, my jade stalk rebelled and refused to perform. But now I desire only one woman, whom I love and with whom I shall spend the rest of my days, my jade stalk is happy and contented, and will perform for me whenever I wish.' These people asking my advice look perplexed. 'Why should love and faithfulness make such a difference to a physical organ?' they ask. 'If the heart is empty of love, then the jade stalk becomes empty of passion', I reply; 'but if the heart is full of love, the jade stalk becomes filled with passion.'

SENGAI

A Zen master in Japan, he was famous for his erotic cartoons. One of the few pictures which survive shows a man laying his outsize penis on an altar, symbolically offering his sex life to God. In his writing he taught that coitus not only brought a man and a woman into union, but could also unify the male and female principles within each person. Thus in a sexual partnership the man and the woman should learn to ignore their respective genders, with the man often playing the passive role and the woman the active role.

Forgetting Gender

Falling in love is dangerous, because passion is an illusion. But being in love gives life flavour. And ultimately the veil of passion becomes the path of enlightenment.

A face like a peach blossom, lips like ripe fruit, and an elegant body trembling with passion, can bring even an old man back to life. And yet young men are frequently frightened by beautiful women.

Remember that the union of men and women is the

source of life itself. So without sexual passion there would be no new human bodies for the souls of the dead to enter.

Sometimes the deepest compassion and the truest love can be found in a prostitute. Do not despise the woman whom other men treat like dirt.

Let a man grow his hair like a woman's; let him shave his face so it is smooth; and put a cloak over his body so its precise shape cannot be seen. That man will be mistaken for a woman. Equally let a woman wear her hair like a man, and let her wear tight clothes that press her breasts flat. That woman will be mistaken for a man. In truth there is no difference between a man and a woman, except for the pleasant way in which the sexual organs are fashioned, so the one fits into the other. And if a man and a woman want to entangle themselves night after night in the red thread of passion, never becoming bored and always remaining potent, they should forget their genders. Let the woman frequently play the man, and let the man frequently play the woman.

TAOISM

INTRODUCTION: TAOISM

The Taoist philosophy of life is symbolized by a circle divided into two pear shapes of black and white, such that the black seems to penetrate the white, and the white penetrates the black; and the black half contains a white dot, and the white half a black dot. The white represents Yang, the male element in all things, and the black represents Yin, the female element; the dots show that all Yang contains Yin, and all Yin contains Yang; and the shape of the black and white halves illustrates that the art of life is to balance Yin and Yang in perfect harmony. The achievement of balance is known as the Tao – the way of harmony.

To the Taoist everything can be understood in terms of Yin and Yang. Yang, the male element, is bright and forceful; thus it predominates in the animals, in mountains, in tall trees, and in heat. Yin, the female element, is dark and receptive, so it is dominant in fish, clouds, valleys and water. Projected onto the universe as a whole, Yang is identified with heaven and Yin with earth.

This philosophy has profound implications for human sexuality. The purpose of sex is not simply to produce children or to receive enjoyment, but to preserve our physical and spiritual health by bringing the Yin and Yang elements into close union. When the man enters the woman heaven is quite literally coming down to earth; and when the woman responds to the man's coital movements, earth is moving in harmony with heaven. Such a high religious view of sex led to ceremonies being held in temples in which, after an elaborate erotic dance, a man and a woman would have sexual intercourse in front of the congregation. The couple acted according to the strict rules laid down by the Taoist sages, and those watching could learn and apply these rules for themselves.

The crux of Taoist sexual teaching is that the man and the woman should concentrate on one another so intently that at every stage they are thinking, feeling and acting in unison. Thus the man should learn to restrain his Yang so that it does not overwhelm the woman's Yin; in particular he should ensure that his passion rises slowly, like the woman's passion, and that even at the height of sexual arousal he should remain in control of himself. The Taoist sexual manuals contain detailed descriptions of the woman's changing physical appearance as her passion is aroused, to enable the man to harmonize his passion with hers. The reward of such harmony is that the man and the woman reach their climax simultaneously, when the man releases his Yang essence and the woman her Yin essence. Not only is this intensely pleasurable, but also by mingling the Yin and Yang essences the man and the woman will receive renewed strength and vitality. According to Taoist teaching, the mixed male and female fluids are reabsorbed by the man and the woman, finding their way back into the brain.

The Taoist sages strongly advocate 'coitus reservatus', in which the man prevents himself from ejaculating either by mental control or by physical technique. The extent to which this should be used depends on the man's age. A young man can ejaculate daily without ill effect, but an older man should ejaculate only weekly or even monthly. The reason is that the man's semen contains his Yang essence; so by releasing it too frequently he will lose his strength and health, and perhaps even die. Yet men, even in old age, are advised to continue enjoying sex as frequently as they are physically able, since, even when they hold back their Yang essence, they will still receive the woman's Yin.

WEI PO-YANG

Writing in the middle of the second century, during the Han dynasty, he was renowned as an alchemist. His most famous work, *The Pact of the Triple Equation*, is mainly concerned with turning lead into mercury. But in discussing the philosophical background to alchemy he touches on numerous other subjects, including sex; and his paragraphs on balance and harmony in sex form the earliest surviving statement of Taoist sexual philosophy.

Balance and Harmony

If Yin and Yang are balanced, then the animal and the spiritual aspects of our nature merge. This gives the ideal condition for conception to occur. The animal part of human nature produces mutual desire, and so coitus is physically possible. The spiritual part of human nature enables the semen to spread out and infuse the woman, causing conception.

During coitus the man should enter the woman nine times. He should withdraw immediately the first three times. On the other six times he should remain inside for an increasing length of time. On the final time he should remain inside, making such movement as is necessary to come to a climax. At the moment the semen enters her, the woman should remain motionless. In this way Yin and Yang are perfectly balanced. This will ensure conception, and cause the child to grow within the womb with strong bones and sinewy muscles.

The seed which the man ejaculates is from Heaven. The woman's womb that receives the seed is of Earth. This conception is the point where Heaven and Earth meet. It is as natural for Heaven to come down to Earth in coitus as for water to run down a hill. It is as natural for Earth to open herself to receive Heaven in coitus as it is for the flame of a fire to reach upwards. Thus when man and woman are united in such a way that coitus is achieved, their actions are in perfect natural harmony. So it requires no special skills that must be taught, but rather the rediscovery of natural inclinations.

TUNG HSUAN

As chief physician to the Chinese emperor early in the seventh century, his views on sexual problems were eagerly sought. Like all Chinese doctors he saw himself simply as the repository of ancient wisdom. And in sexual matters he passed on the teaching of the 'Dark Girl', a mystical figure who instructed the first Chinese emperor in the arts of sex. His lengthy treatise is the classic Taoist sex manual to which all later works defer.

The Philosophy of Sexual Union

Of all the ten thousand things created by Heaven, Man is the most precious. Of all the things that can make man flourish, none is greater than sexual union. It reflects the glory of Heaven, and it is rooted in Earth. It regulates Yin and Yang. Those who understand and practise it correctly can enhance their health and prolong their lives. Those who miss its true meaning will damage their health, and die before their time.

The methods of coitus taught by the Dark Girl have been passed from one sage to another since ancient times.

The wisest men on Earth have sought to explain its subtle mysteries and its finer nuances. They have described how the man and the woman should sit and lie together; the postures that give variety and satisfaction; the methods of thrusting and of penetration; and the way in which these techniques bring Yin and Yang into balance. Those who have obeyed these ancient teachings have attained pleasure and lived into old age. Those who have ignored the ancient teachings have not been satisfied and have died young. The purpose of this treatise is to pass the wisdom of the sages to future generations.

In the natural order of things Heaven moves and Earth responds. Thus we see heaven revolving to the right, and Earth responding by revolving to the left, causing the four seasons to follow one after the other. In coitus the man is Heaven and the woman is Earth. Thus if the man moves and the woman does not respond, or if the woman is roused but the man is not the cause of her arousal, the sexual act will injure both the man and the woman. In this situation they should abstain from coitus. If, however, the man shows his desire for the woman, and the woman's desire is thereby stimulated, then they are in harmony with the cosmic pattern, and sexual union should ensue. And throughout coitus the man's movements and the woman's responses should be in harmony, to reflect the harmony of Heaven and Earth. In this way Yin and Yang will be perfectly balanced.

It must be remembered that, while Heaven moves and Earth responds, the forces of Earth can be stronger than the forces of Heaven. Thus in sexual matters the woman, while she responds to the man's movements, can be stronger in her passion and her constitution than the man. Man and woman may be compared with fire and water. Fire can be fanned so it quickly burns hot and bright, but it can also burn itself out quickly. Water itself is slow to warm, and slow to cool, and if too much water is put on the fire, the flames are soon extinguished. Thus the man's passion is quickly aroused, yet it can quickly subside, while the woman's passion is slow to be aroused and slow to subside. And, strange as it may seem, if the woman's passion exceeds the man's, the man's potency may dwindle and his jade stalk become soft and flaccid.

Here then is the hardest lesson that man and woman should learn. If Yin and Yang are to be balanced, the man and the woman must harmonize their passion. The man must restrain his passion so that it rises with the woman's passion; thus his movements must be such that the woman can respond. Equally when the woman's passion is fully aroused, she must not overwhelm the man, bringing him to a premature climax. If the man's movements and the woman's responses are in disharmony, it is the man who will suffer most, because his constitution is weaker. But if in the sexual act Heaven and Earth are in harmony, and hence Yin and Yang are perfectly balanced, the man and the woman will shine with health.

Yin and Yang Rising Together

When the man and the woman come together, the man should sit down at the woman's left side and the woman should sit on the man's right. Then the man should turn his head to look at the woman, his head revolving to the right as Heaven does; and the woman should turn to the man, her head revolving to the left, as Earth does. Their eyes should linger on one another, enjoying the beauty of each other's body.

Now the man crosses his legs and the woman sits on his lap. He presses her waist, and caresses her body, moving his hands up and down, and round and round. He should not at this time touch her most sensitive parts as she is not ready. He whispers words of love, describing the feelings within him, and uplifting her with compliments. As her passion rises, she whispers words of love, describing her feelings. He puts his arms round her body, and draws her to him so their breasts and their bellies meet.

They press their lips together. At first their lips are firm and their mouths closed. Then she opens her mouth a little, to indicate that she is ready for more intimacy. He sucks her lower lip, and she sucks his upper lip. They feed on one another's saliva. He softly bites her tongue, and, placing his hands on her head, pinches her ears. By this kissing and caressing a thousand charms will unfold and a hundred sorrows be forgotten.

The man finds that his jade stalk is becoming hard and

erect, and he will find the Yang essence rising within his body and surging towards the jade stalk. Similarly the Yin essence will be stimulated within the woman and surge towards her vulva, making it moist. This is a spontaneous response of Yin and Yang that could never be achieved by rational thought, but only by the right loving actions. Once they have reached this stage the man and the woman are ready for sexual union.

Many men make the mistake of allowing the Yang essence to rise too quickly, and so reach a fever of desire while the woman is only starting to warm. Such haste is not natural, and results from ignorance. Within each man, although the Yang essence dominates, the Yin essence is also present. It is natural therefore for the Yin to temper the Yang, and so the man's sexual passion rises in harmony with the woman, each becoming ready for union at the same time.

Equally some women remain cold, despite the man's loving actions, and so the Yin essence remains dormant. This too is unnatural, and results from ignorance. Within each woman, although the Yin essence dominates, the Yang essence is also present. It is natural, therefore, for the Yang to stimulate the Yin, releasing its power, so the woman responds fully to the man.

Positions and Variations

Careful investigation has shown that there are four basic positions for consummating the sexual union, and there are twenty variations. These encompass all possibilities, and have from ancient times been given special names. If a man and a woman understand and practise them, they will discover for themselves their wonderful meaning.

The four basic positions are known as Close Union, Unicorn Horn, Firm Attachment, and Exposed Gills.

Close Union has eleven variations:

i.   Silkworm Spinning a Cocoon. The woman with both hands clasps the man's neck. Then with both her legs she clasps him at the base of his back or buttocks.

ii.   Winding Dragon. The man, using his left hand, pushes back the woman's legs so that her knees approach her breasts. Using his right hand, he guides his jade stalk into her jade gate.

iii.   Pair of Swallows. The man lies flat upon the woman, his stomach on hers, his breast on hers, and she embraces his waist.

iv.   Union of Kingfishers. The woman lies on her back and opens her legs. The man kneels between her legs, takes her by the waist, and lifts her towards him.

v.   Low Pine Tree. The woman lies on her back and the man comes down on to her. She crosses her legs around his waist.

vi.   Flying Seagulls. The woman lies on the bed, with her legs dangling over the side. The man stands at the side of the bed and holds her legs at either side of him.

vii.   Gambolling Wild Horses. The woman lies on her back and the man kneels between her legs. She then lifts her legs onto his shoulders, presenting her jade gate to his jade stalk.

viii. Galloping Steed. The woman lies on her back and the man kneels. He lifts her buttocks onto his lap, and then lifts her body towards his body, so that she is sitting on him, held by his strength.

ix.   Horse's Hooves. The woman lies on her back. He puts one of her feet onto his shoulder, and leaves the other one dangling.

x.   Phoenix Playing in a Cave. The woman lies on her back, and holds both legs in the air with her own hands.

xi.   Giant Bird Soaring over the Sea. The woman lies on her back, and the man kneels. She lifts her legs onto his upper arms. Then he clasps her by the waist and pulls her towards him.

Unicorn Horn has three variations:

i.   Flying Ducks. The man lies on his back. The woman squats over him, facing his feet, and lowers her jade gate onto his jade stalk.

ii.   Singing Monkey Embracing a Tree. The man sits on a stool or on the floor. The woman sits facing him on his lap. She embraces him, while he supports her buttocks.

iii.   Cat and Mouse in One Hole. The man lies on his back. The woman lies on top of him, face to face.

Firm Attachment has only one form:

i.   Two Fishes. The man lies on the woman, face to face.
      She opens her legs so his jade stalk can enter her jade
      gate. They kiss deeply.

Exposed Gills has five variations:

i.   Mandarin Ducks. The woman lies on her side, and
      curls her legs towards her stomach. The man lies
      behind her, and inserts his jade stalk from the
      rear.
ii.   Jumping White Tiger. The woman kneels, bending
      forwards so that her palms are on the floor. The man
      kneels behind her, holding her by the waist.
iii. Dark Cicada Clinging to a Tree. The woman lies face
      down on her stomach, and spreads her legs. The man
      lies on top of her, his stomach on her back, holding
      her shoulders.
iv.   Goat Facing a Tree. The man sits on a chair. The
      woman sits on him with her back to his face, while he
      holds her by the waist.
v.   Donkeys in Late Spring. The woman stands up
      and bends over, supporting herself on a chair or
      against a wall. The man stands behind her, holding
      her waist.

The Art of the Jade Stalk

There are six ways in which the jade stalk may penetrate.

i.   Pushing the jade stalk in, and moving it forwards and backwards. This may be compared with a saw in a piece of wood.

ii.   Pushing the jade stalk down, and then pulling it up by the golden gully (the clitoris), as if one were slicing off stones to find the beautiful jade.

iii. Aiming the jade stalk in the direction of the golden gully, like an iron pestle pounding medicine in a mortar.

iv.   Moving the jade stalk in and out and from side to side, like a blacksmith sharpening iron with a hammer.

v.   Jabbing the jade stalk with quick short thrusts, like the farmer hoeing his land for late planting.

vi.   Pushing the jade stalk through the jade gate very slowly and carefully, as if one were opening an oyster shell. Then gently go deeper as if one were searching for a pearl.

There are nine ways of moving the jade stalk.

i.   Striking out to the left and right, like a brave warrior breaking up the enemy ranks.

ii.   Moving up and down like a wild horse bucking through a stream.

iii. Pulling out and pushing in, like a group of seagulls playing in the waves.

iv.   Alternating deep and shallow thrusts swiftly,
      like a sparrow picking rice grain that has been left
      over in a mortar.

v.   Making a number of gentle, shallow thrusts,
      followed by a deep thrust, like a large stone sinking
      in the sea.

vi.   Pushing inwards very, very slowly, like a snake
      entering a hole to hibernate.

vii. Pushing inwards very, very quickly, like a
      frightened mouse entering a hole.

viii. Remain stationary, with the jade stalk at the jade
      gate, then push swiftly, like an eagle sweeping
      down to catch a hare.

ix.   Rising up and then plunging deeply, like a big ship
      rising and plunging in the waves.

Achieving Conception

The man who desires a child should wait until after the
woman has menstruated. If he copulates with her on the
first to third day after menstruation has ceased, he will
obtain a son. If he copulates with her on the fourth or fifth
day, a girl will be conceived. All emissions of semen
after the fifth day are wasted, because no child will
be conceived. On those occasions when conception is
possible, it will only occur if the man emits his semen at
exactly the same time as the woman reaches orgasm.

A child conceived at midnight will live to an advanced
age. A child conceived before midnight will reach a normal
age. A child conceived after midnight will not live long.

To increase the possibility of conception, the man and the woman at the point of orgasm should orientate their bodies according to the cosmic forces. In the spring, their heads should point east; in summer, south; in autumn, west; and in winter, north.

FANG NEI CHI

W riting shortly after Tung Hsuan, he composed a
dialogue between the Dark Girl and the Yellow
Emperor, in which she gradually reveals the mysteries of
sex in answer to his questions. The Emperor is anxious
about his poor health, which she attributes to errors in
his sexual behaviour. His sexual potency is also failing,
and she teaches him how to restore both health and
virility.

The Secret of Life

The Yellow Emperor said to the Dark Girl: 'My spirit is
weak and in disharmony, my heart is sad and constantly
anxious. What should I do about this?'

The Dark Girl replied: 'All such feebleness can be
attributed to sexual errors. Those who are expert in sexual
intercourse are like good cooks who know how to blend
the individual flavours into a tasty dish. You must learn to
blend correctly Yin and Yang in your sexual activities.
Then your heart and spirit will be healed, and you will
live long. But if you fail to blend Yin and Yang correctly,

you will not truly enjoy sexual intercourse; and your health will gradually decline.'

The Yellow Emperor, still looking sad and anxious, nodded for the Dark Girl to continue her discourse: 'A man can live long if he conserves his semen and thus sustains his spirit. He may eat a healthy diet and take the right medicines; but if he does not know and practise the right method of sexual intercourse, food and drugs will be useless. The union of man and woman is like the union of Heaven and Earth. It is because they are correctly unified that Heaven and Earth last for ever. Mankind has lost the secret of union, and so his life gradually ebbs away. If, however, a man can rediscover this secret, and achieve perfect balance between Yin and Yang, he will attain immortality.'

The Yellow Emperor then asked the Dark Girl: 'What happens if a man decides to refrain entirely from sexual intercourse?'

The Dark Girl answered: 'This is wrong. Heaven and Earth have times when they are open to each other and times when they are closed; so too men and women must sometimes be open to each other, and sometimes closed. During the sexual act the vital essences of Yin and Yang are blended, and so the spirits of both the man and the woman are revitalized. If the jade stalk becomes totally inactive a man will die. But its activity should be controlled and guided. If a man learns the art of copulating without emitting semen, then the semen will be enriched, and return to his spirit. This is the secret of life itself.'

Harmonizing the Mood

The Yellow Emperor said to the Dark Girl: 'There are times when my jade stalk fails to rise. The sight of the woman's body fails to excite me, and I feel no surge of life within me. The woman laughs at my limp and powerless jade stalk, and I am deeply humiliated. What should I do on such occasions?'

The Dark Girl replied: 'Though each man believes he suffers alone, the problem which Your Majesty describes is very common. The problem occurs when the emotions of the man and woman are not in harmony. Thus even though there may be a strong desire for coitus, the conflict of spirit makes this impossible.'

The Yellow Emperor then said: 'How can I ensure that my spirit and that of the woman are in harmony, so that my jade stalk rises and coitus is possible?'

The Dark Girl answered: 'You must learn to ignore your jade stalk. The fear which you have of your jade stalk failing to rise so absorbs your spirit that you are unable to respond to the woman's spirit. Only if you concentrate on the woman will your jade stalk be free. You must not be impatient and fast, but patient and slow. Engage in loving conversation, so that through your words Yin and Yang may begin to blend. Then begin to kiss and caress, at all times observing the woman's response, so that your movements make complementary movements in her. And as she is aroused, you too will be aroused: the vital essence will surge towards your jade stalk and her vulva at the same time.'

The Yellow Emperor went on to ask a further question: 'There are times when a man wishes to copulate with a woman, his jade stalk fully erect, but she is not aroused: her vulva is so dry that the jade stalk cannot easily enter. What is the cause of this?'

The Dark Girl replied: 'The cause is the same: the emotions of the man and the woman are not in harmony. Yin and Yang are mutually dependent. When Yang does not obtain Yin, it is sad and cannot be active: this is what is happening when the jade stalk cannot rise. When Yin cannot obtain Yang, it is sad and cannot be active: this is what is happening when the vulva remains dry and closed. If under these circumstances the man and the woman try to have intercourse, they will become ill, and may even destroy their capacity for intercourse in the future. Thus intercourse should only occur when Yin and Yang are perfectly blended, and thus the spirits of the man and the woman are in harmony.'

Observing the Woman

The Yellow Emperor asked the Dark Girl: 'How can a man judge the depth and the strength of a woman's desire?'

The Dark Girl replied: 'A woman has five desires, and each desire manifests itself in a different way. First, there is desire of the mind: when her thoughts are filled with desire, her breathing becomes fast and irregular. Second, there is desire of the vulva: when she want him to enter, her nostrils distend and her mouth opens. Third, there is desire of the Yin essence: when the tide of Yin is surging through her body, she begins to shake and she holds the man's body tightly. Fourth, there is desire of the body: when her body is totally filled with desire, she perspires copiously. Fifth, there is desire of the orgasmic spirit: when she is about to reach orgasm, she stretches her body and closes her eyes.'

The Yellow Emperor wanted to know how he could fully satisfy a woman: 'Even if a man becomes adept at observing the various desires of a woman, how can he act to give her complete satisfaction?'

The Dark Girl replied: 'The man must also observe carefully the movements of the woman's body, for each movement is a sign to the man. There are ten movements. First, she clasps the man tightly with both hands, indicating she wishes him to press his body closely to hers. Second, she raises her legs, indicating she wants faster thrusts of his jade stalk. Third, she stretches her body, pulling her vulva slightly away from him, which indicates she wants shallower thrusts. Fourth, she uses her feet like hooks to pull the man closer to her, indicating she wants deeper thrusts. Fifth, she shakes from side to side, indicating she wishes him to thrust alternately on the left and the right. Sixth, she crosses her legs over his body, indicating she wants more of what he has been doing. Seventh, she relaxes her body, indicating that she wishes him to stop thrusting for a few moments. Eighth, her jade gate locks on to his jade stalk, indicating she wishes him to remain deep inside without moving. Ninth, her thighs start to twitch and move, indicating she wishes him to resume thrusting. Tenth, she lifts her body upwards, pressing against him, which indicates her climax is near.'

The Yellow Emperor asked: 'How can the man know that the woman is fulfilled?'

The Dark Girl replied: 'The woman indicates fulfilment when her body and limbs relax completely, and a red patch appears on her breast. Then the man must cease his activity.'

Controlling Ejaculation

The Yellow Emperor said to the Dark Girl: 'Many men say that the pleasure of coitus lies in the emission of semen at the moment of climax. Is this true or false?'

The Dark Girl replied: 'Such an idea is both false and dangerous. After the emission of semen the man's body is tired, his ears are buzzing, his eyes are heavy with sleep, his throat is parched and his limbs are weak. Although he has experienced a brief moment of joy, no pleasure remains. But if a man has coitus without ejaculating, his vital essence is strengthened, his body remains vigorous, and his hearing and vision are acute. By holding back his passion at the moment of climax, his love for the woman is increased, and he continues to desire her.'

The Yellow Emperor asked: 'It is said that frequent coitus improves a man's health. Is this true or false?'

The Dark Girl replied: ''It is true or false depending on a man's ability to control ejaculation. If a man has intercourse frequently, and on each occasion emits semen, his vital essence will dissipate, and he will become weak and ill. But if he has intercourse frequently without emitting semen, his vital essence will grow strong, his hearing and vision will be acute, his body will resist diseases, and his soul will be at peace. Others will be able to observe his good health because his complexion will shine. There are men of a great age with perfect control of ejaculation who are able to engage in the sexual act ten times a day, and at the end of the day he will be stronger and more vigorous than at the beginning.'

The Yellow Emperor asked: 'How is it possible to control ejaculation?'

The Dark Girl replied: 'When a man feels that he might soon lose control, he should withdraw his jade stalk, until only the tip is within the jade gate, and stay in that position without moving. Then he should breathe deeply, using his diaphragm rather than his chest to draw breath; and at the same time he should contract his lower abdomen as if he were controlling the urge to defecate. All the while he should think of the importance to his health of conserving his vital essence.'

The Yellow Emperor asked: 'What should a man do if he feels this method of control will fail?'

The Dark Girl replied: 'The technique he should use is like stopping the Yellow River with one's hand. He must quickly and firmly press with the three middle fingers of his left hand on the spot between his scrotum and his anus, inhaling deeply and gnashing his teeth. If he is so excited that even this fails to work, he should withdraw his jade stalk completely from the woman, seize the top of it between his thumb and forefinger and squeeze: then the Yellow River will surely be stopped. He will feel his vital essence go back into his body and towards his brain.'

The Yellow Emperor asked: 'How frequently can a man allow himself to reach a full climax and emit his semen without endangering his health?'

The Dark Girl replied: 'The answer is different for strong men and weak men, for young and old. Every man must regulate his emissions according to the condition of his vital essence. Strong men of fifteen years can afford to emit semen twice a day; thin, weak men of the same age only once a day. By the time the strong man reaches thirty years, he too should emit semen only once a day, while the weak man should confine himself to once every two days. Strong men of forty can emit semen once in three days, weak men once in six days. Strong men of fifty once in five days, weak men once in ten days. Strong men of sixty once in ten days, weak men once in twenty days. Strong men of seventy or more should emit semen only once a month, while weak men of that age should never emit semen.'

The Yellow Emperor asked: 'Should the frequency of emission vary with the seasons?'

The Dark Girl replied: 'The guidance I have given is for the spring, when the vital essence is strongest. In the summer and autumn the wise man emits semen less often. And in winter, when the vital essence is weakest, many wise men refuse to emit semen at all. Each man, if he has the wisdom to meditate on the matter, can judge for himself how frequently he can safely emit semen.'

Exchanging Vital Essence

The Yellow Emperor asked: 'By controlling ejaculation a man conserves his vital essence. How through coitus can his vital essence be increased?'

The Dark Girl replied: 'The purpose of intercourse is for the Yin and the Yang to become perfectly balanced; and this requires that the man and the woman should let their vital essences intermingle, and so each gains the vital essence of the other. This is especially important when the man emits semen, because in doing so he is giving much of his vital essence to the woman. Thus to compensate he must absorb much of the woman's vital essence.'

The Yellow Emperor asked: 'How is it possible for the vital essences to intermingle, and each to gain from the other?'

The Dark Girl replied: 'When a man's stalk enters the jade gate and he starts to thrust, moisture from both the man and the woman is stimulated; the two forms of moisture mix to form a liquid in which Yin and Yang are balanced. As thrusting continues, both the man and the woman absorb the mixed moisture, and at the same time more moisture is stimulated. Thus the longer intercourse continues, the greater will be the mixing of moisture, and hence the greater will be the benefits.'

The Yellow Emperor asked: 'Are there ways in which the exchange of vital essence can be even greater?'

The Dark Girl answered: 'There are two ways in which the intermingling of vital essence is most greatly enhanced. The first is through kissing. The man and the woman should open their mouths, and press their mouths tightly together so that no air can escape; then the man should breathe inwards while the woman breathes outwards, followed by the man breathing outwards while the woman breathes inwards. By inhaling each other's breath they exchange vital essence. They should also spit and suck each other's saliva. The second way is for the woman to suck the man's jade stalk, and the man to suck the woman's jade gate. They should only do this when thrusting has made the jade stalk and the jade gate very moist.'

CHUNG HO

Like Wei Po-Yang, he was an alchemist who also pronounced on sexual matters, seeing sexual fulfilment, like successful alchemy, as depending on the balance of Yin and Yang. His date is unknown, and his original treatise is lost, but he is quoted in later works.

A Warning against Selfishness

Men and women who are selfish in sexual matters can often do great harm to their partners. For example, there was once a beautiful queen of the western kingdom who wished to obtain immortality by nurturing her Yin essence. Every time she had coitus she would suck the man until his whole mouth was dry, and she would induce him to ejaculate quickly. In this way she took his Yang essence which enhanced her Yin essence. But she gave nothing to the man, not sharing her saliva with him, and producing only enough moisture at her jade gate to allow his jade stalk to enter. As a result all her partners became weak and ill, and many died. The same happens if a man takes all for himself, sucking the woman's mouth and jade gate dry, but giving nothing in return.

Yet such selfishness ultimately destroys its perpetrator. For a few years the queen of the western kingdom glowed with health, her complexion pink and shiny. But then her system became so full of vital essences that her body and her limbs became bloated, until finally she could hardly move. Many selfish men and women have suffered the same fate.

SUN SZU-MO

A famous Taoist physician, he wrote the most popular of all sex manuals. He entitled it *A Healthy Sex Life* and dedicated it to the emperor late in the seventh century. Initially it only circulated in court circles, but four centuries later it was printed and distributed throughout China and beyond. Much of it repeats the advice of earlier manuals. But its particular focus is the continuation of sexual activity into old age.

The Art of the Bedchamber

Until a man reaches the age of forty, he is usually full of vigorous passion. But once he has passed his fortieth year he will notice that his potency starts to diminish. At the same time he becomes much more susceptible to diseases, which may descend upon him like a swarm of bees. If he does nothing to conserve his potency, he will grow steadily weaker until he is beyond cure.

The man's only remedy is to learn and practise the ancient Art of the Bedchamber. This Art, if learned thoroughly, can enable even an old man to copulate ten times in a single night.

A young man, ignorant of this art, engages in coitus to satisfy his lust, exercising no control over his passions. An older man must never give way to lust, but should regard coitus as the means of conserving and enhancing the vital essence. This means that he should emit his semen only on rare occasions, learning to enjoy sexual coitus without the need to reach orgasm.

Yang is modelled after fire, Yin after water. Just as water can quench fire, so Yin can diminish Yang. If coitus lasts too long, or is too frequent, the Yin essence, absorbed by the man from the woman, will become stronger than his own Yang essence, and he will be harmed. What the man gains through the sexual act will be outweighed by what he loses. Thus the Art of the Bedchamber consists also in the man judging correctly how long coitus should last and how frequently he should engage in it.

The Art of the Bedchamber, like any art, depends on a vivid imagination. As the man approaches the woman, he should imagine that just below his stomach there is a bright liquid gushing through him, red and white on the surface and yellow beneath. Then he should imagine the liquid dividing itself, a red stream going up one side of his body and a white stream going up the other side, meeting in his brain. Thus the brain, where his Yang essence resides, and the base of the stomach, to which the Yang essence surges when he is sexually aroused, are united. It is from the base of the stomach that the Yang essence enters the jade stalk, causing it to rise. The brain, through the imaginary red and white streams, now has perfect control of the jade stalk, determining the degree of sexual passion.

A man should beware, however, of exerting this control too harshly. If he never allows his passion to be fully aroused, and so never emits semen, he will become bloated and develop sores and ulcers, as the excess of Yang essence pours out of his body.

Questions and Answers

A peasant aged seventy came to consult me, saying: 'For several days my Yang essence has been most exuberant, so that I want to have coitus with my wife in the daytime as well as at night, reaching orgasm every time. Is this good or bad at my advanced age?'

I answered: 'This is most unfortunate. You know what happens with an oil lamp: just before the wick is burnt out, it suddenly flares up. This sudden flaring up of sexual passion in you will last only a short time, before you are utterly exhausted and become incapable of any sexual activity. Worse still, you may destroy your health, so that within a few weeks you may die. If you wish to survive, there may still be time to curb your passion, and engage in the kind of sexual activity that is appropriate for your age. You should not emit semen more than once a month. And if you find yourself incapable of coitus without emitting semen, you should abstain altogether.'

A man aged sixty asked me: 'Have I reached the age when I should give up sexual activity with my wife?'

I answered: 'If you and your wife have minds that are serene and peaceful, untroubled by thoughts of sex, then it is right that you should abstain from coitus. In this way you shall both live to a great age. But if your minds are restive, often troubled by lustful passion, then it would be most dangerous to abstain. You will find it impossible to sleep soundly, and your urine will become poisonous and turgid, indicating that your whole system is becoming ill. The general rule is that a man and a woman should have coitus with whatever frequency is necessary to give their minds peace.'

A young man came to me, saying: 'I am filled with passion. I have a wife, but I desire variety, and want sexual union with many women. What should I do?'

I answered: 'There are those who say it is good to absorb the Yin essence from many different women, as this will give greater strength to a man's Yang essence. This is a profound error. The Yin essence is the same in every woman, and the Yang in every man. Thus no benefit is gained from coitus with different women. More importantly, it is vital that even young men begin to learn the Art of the Bedchamber; and this is best achieved with one woman who is faithful and loyal, and so wants to assist the man in learning the Art. Thus you must be faithful and loyal to your wife.'

ANCIENT EGYPT

INTRODUCTION: ANCIENT EGYPT

According to the mythology of ancient Egypt, the world was created when the sun masturbated, producing air and water. These two had intercourse, giving birth to the earth, which is male, and the sky, which is female. The sky arched her back over the earth, then lowered herself until she touched him. This union between sky and earth produced life.

The most striking aspect of this story is the sexual superiority of the woman, symbolized by the sky. This is reflected in a religious ceremony described by Herodotus, a Greek traveller to Egypt, in the fifth century BC. Large boats containing equal numbers of men and women were rowed out into the middle of the Nile. Then the women stood up, undressed, and taunted the men for their impotency; the men were required to sit back passively and receive these insults. The purpose was to show that it is the man's job to satisfy the woman, rather than vice versa; and when the boats returned to shore, the men went to the temple to pray for sufficient potency to satisfy their women's desire.

Female superiority is illustrated in the erotic art which

survives. When the man and woman are lying face to face, it is usually the woman who is on top. The man is shown kneeling in front of the woman, kissing her vulva or breasts, or massaging her feet. The most popular position, according to pictures, is where both are standing up; and the woman is usually taller than the man, and apparently taking the initiative.

In the erotic poetry of ancient Egypt the man is normally the supplicant. In one poem he is poor and uneducated, and she rich and sophisticated; nonetheless her desire for him proves stronger than the barriers of class. In another he is a worshipper and she is a goddess. Yet in the most beautiful love poem the woman is compared with the various fruits and trees of the orchard, which the man can enjoy as he wishes.

There was little distinction between religion and sex. Sex was regarded as a religious act, and almost all religious ritual had a strong erotic dimension. Special respect was given to sexual dreams, which were regarded as vehicles of divine prophecy.

Poor Man, Rich Woman

MAN:

There is no-one like you.
You are more beautiful than any other woman.
You are like the star goddess
Arising at the start of the year.
Your skin is bright,
Your eyes shine,

Your lips are full,
Your hair is like lapis lazuli,
Your hands are like lotus flowers,
Your waist is slim,
And your buttocks are heavy.
Your slender legs are fast and agile,
All men turn to look at you.

WOMAN:

My brother disapproves of you.
He says you are poor and ignorant.
My mother shouts at me,
'Stop seeing that horrid man.'
Yet my heart is yours.
Whenever I think of you
My whole body trembles.
I long to embrace you,
To feel you inside me.
The gods themselves seem to say
'Give yourself to him.'
Am I mad?
Have I left my senses?
Surely my mother can see your beauty,
Surely my brother can rejoice at my joy.

MAN:

If only I was rich,
I could impress your family
With gifts of jewels and gold.
I would purchase their approval.
If only I was royal,
I could imprison all
Who opposed our love.
But your brother is right,
I am poor and ignorant.
I live by hard, sweaty work.
I know nothing beyond the ways
Of growing crops and tending livestock.
Have I the right
To ask you to run away
From your brother and mother?
And if I asked,
Would you come?

WOMAN:

I walked past your hovel.
The door was open, and I looked in.
I could see you sitting.
You were so handsome,
So elegant and beautiful
In the dim half-light.
Yet others regard you as rough,
Smelling of soil and animal dung.

If I was to buy you fine clothes,
Would you wear them?
If I was to purchase sweet perfume,
Would you use it?

MAN:

I would jump the moon for you.
I would swing in the stars for you.
I would swim the length of the Nile for you.
I would work day and night for you.
But I cannot deceive for you.
I cannot pretend to be someone else.
The man you love
Is poor, ignorant and rough.
If I was to look fine and smell sweet
Your brother and mother might approve.
But your love would melt away.
You love me as I am,
For what I am.

WOMAN:

You are right.
I despair.
I want to love you,
To give my heart to you,
To share my body with you.
And yet I must be loyal
To the mother that bore me,

To the brother that feeds me.
What can be done?

MAN:

The man in love is a god,
The woman in love a goddess.
We possess in our hearts
Power beyond our imagination.
We are not bound
By the deathly rules of status.
In the eyes of others
You are high and I am low.
In the eyes of love
We are both high,
Higher than the highest king.
A god and a goddess
Can unite their sexual organs
For all eternity,
And their joy is infinite.
So let us behave
Like the beings we are.
Let my hovel be our heaven,
Let my bed be our cloud,
On which we are united
In perfect, heavenly bliss.

WOMAN:

For days, for weeks, for months,
I have been sick for love.
No medicine could cure me.
My mother and my brother
Thought I would surely die.
Yet they preferred my death
To our love.
Now I have returned to life.
I am well and strong,
Because I am a goddess.
I will come to your heaven,
And lie on your cloud.
In perfect pleasure
We shall float high above the earth.
My bliss will make me kind,
So I shall let rain fall
From our heavenly cloud
Onto my brother's crops.

I Wish

I wish I were your doorkeeper
So that I could stand guard against other men.
I want you only for myself.

I wish I were your slave
So that I could serve you in your room.
I want always to be with you.

121

I wish I were your laundryman
So that I could wash your fragrant garments.
I want to smell your body's aroma.

I wish I were your mirror
So that I could look at your face.
I want to stare at your beauty.

I wish I were your signet ring
So that I would always be touching you.
I want to feel the sweat of your hand.

I wish I were the water in your bath
So that I could embrace your whole body.
I want to feel your neck, your breasts, your lips.

I wish I were your sandals
So that you would step on me as you walked.
I want to feel your weight on my body.

You are my goddess, and I your worshipper.
In loving you, I love all divinity.
I live for you, and I will die for you.

Love in the Orchard

The pomegranate opens its mouth, and says:
'My seeds are like her teeth.
My fruits are like her breasts.
I am the best fruit in the orchard
Because I endure through every season.

122

You can pluck me and enjoy me
In every month of the year.'

The fig-tree opens its mouth, and says:
'My juice is like her saliva,
Sweet to the taste of her lover.
I am the best fruit in the orchard
Because I give the greatest pleasure.
You can pick me and suck me,
And never be disappointed.'

The sycamore tree opens its mouth, and says:
'My branches are like her arms,
And my trunk is like her body.
I am the best tree in the orchard
Because you can come to me at any time
And relax in my embrace,
Which is cool in the heat of the day.'

The god of every fruit and every tree
Is a god of love.
The whole orchard sings
Of the heavenly pleasure of love.
Come to the orchard and love me.
Our pleasure shall be their joy.
The gods themselves will rejoice
As they witness our passion.

As we walk in the orchard hand in hand
My whole body trembles with desire.
To hear your voice whispering words of love
Is like drinking the sweetest pomegranate wine.

As we lie down amidst the fragrant herbs
I touch your thighs, your lips, your breasts,
And kiss your open lips with my open mouth.
Is this the sport of gods?
Is this the heaven they promise?

A Man's Prophetic Dreams

If he dreams his penis becomes large, his wealth will multiply.

If he has intercourse with his mother, his companions will stick with him.

If he has intercourse with his sister, he will inherit something.

If he has intercourse with a rat, a judgement will be passed against him.

If his penis becomes erect, he will be robbed.

If he has intercourse with a falcon, he will also be robbed.

If he shaves his pubic hairs, a loved one will die.

If he sees a woman's vulva, great misery will come upon him.

If he has intercourse with a pig, he will lose his wealth.

If he has intercourse with his wife in the sun, the gods will have mercy on him and bless him.

A Woman's Prophetic Dreams

If a mouse has intercourse with her, her husband will be a fine lover.

If a horse has intercourse with her, her husband will be a violent lover.

If a peasant has intercourse with her, her husband will be kind and considerate.

If a donkey has intercourse with her, she will be punished for a great sin.

If a goat has intercourse with her, she will die soon.

If a wolf has intercourse with her, she will see something beautiful.

If a serpent has intercourse with her, her husband will become cruel.

If a baboon has intercourse with her, she will become kind and benevolent.

If a bird has intercourse with her, another woman will try to seduce her husband.

If a married woman has intercourse with her, she will turn against her husband.

If a stranger has intercourse with her, she will leave her home and never return.

If a son has intercourse with her, that son will perish.

GREECE
AND ROME

INTRODUCTION:
GREECE AND ROME

According to Greek mythology, Cronos, son of heaven and earth, castrated his father with a billhook and threw his testicles into the sea. Semen poured from the testicles, causing the sea to be covered in a white foam. Out of this foam emerged Aphrodite, the goddess of sexual intercourse. She in turn, through her union with Hermes, gave birth to Hermaphroditos, who had both breasts and a penis; and through her union with Dionysus, to Priapus, a male divinity whose penis was permanently erect.

The supernatural world contained in the works of Homer, Plutarch, Hesiod and the other epic poets – the story of Aphrodite and her offspring is from Hesiod's *Theogony* – is filled with divine sexual encounters in which potency and valour, rather than love and fidelity, are the primary virtues; rarely does one sense any emotional warmth between god and goddess. The human heroes were equally lusty. Heracles, admired by all Greeks for his courage, strength and tenacity, ravished fifty virgins in a single night; and also had frequent homosexual affairs with pretty teenage boys, including his own nephew.

Since these were the stories that fed childish imaginations in ancient Greece, it is hardly surprising that sexual relationships, as recounted in contemporary descriptions, lacked tenderness and artistry. Marriage was regarded by most Greek men as a necessary social obligation, and intercourse between husband and wife was usually a hurried, loveless business, whose sole purpose was procreation. As the commentator Demosthenes wrote: 'We have prostitutes for our pleasure, concubines for our daily needs, and wives to give us legitimate children and look after the house.' He could have added masturbation as another means of satisfying daily needs, since Greek literature abounds in descriptions of the aids which both men and women used to give themselves pleasure. The only sexual relationship which was respected for its emotional, as well as physical, joy was that between the wise teacher and his teenage pupil. Socrates himself regarded the love which an older man felt for the pubescent boys in his charge as the most exalted human emotion; and numerous pictures survive of such men buggering their pupils.

Roman civilization, in sexual as in other matters, sought to emulate Greek culture, with only minor differences. The Romans, with some notable exceptions, were rampantly heterosexual, regarding homosexual liaisons with suspicion. And wives enjoyed more freedom and respect. Indeed on one occasion in the second century BC women actually mobbed the Senate demanding the right to own property for themselves. Yet female liberty did not bear fruit in greater tenderness between men and women.

So in the great corpus of classical Greek and Roman literature, there is very little where religious and sexual feelings unite. Many centuries after the demise of Greek civilization Constantine Cephalas made an anthology of Greek love poetry and epigrams. Much of the material is rather cynical or crude, but there are occasional poems of great tenderness and beauty – including four poems by a man who, after many years of wandering, has rediscovered his love for his wife.

The greatest Latin poet, Ovid, devoted considerable attention to sexual matters; and, though the morals he espoused were dubious, his love lyrics do at times contain great spiritual, as well as sexual, wisdom. Arguably the erotic works of Catullus, his older contemporary, are even finer, and are certainly more tender.

CONSTANTINE CEPHALUS

In the tenth century AD, over a thousand years after the decline of ancient Greek civilization, he made a collection of all the erotic Greek writings he could find. Much of it is anonymous, and its origins obscure. For many centuries the collection, known discreetly as the *Greek Anthology*, was privately circulated amongst scholars.

Lessons of Love

I have wandered through the lands of love
And I have learnt hard lessons there.
Avoid the streets, for the women there are cold,
They think of nothing but the money you will give.
Pleasure with them leads only to disgust.
Avoid young virgins, full of innocent hope.
They think of nothing but domestic bliss,
Which I have learnt is a cruel illusion.
Avoid your neighbour's wife, even when she smiles at you:
In the end her husband will discover her sin
And his anger will be poured out on you.
Avoid widows: either they are filled only with lust,

132

And have no desire for the gentler arts of love,
Or else they want marriage and your money.
Avoid your servant girls or slaves:
Once you have loved her she will never respect you,
And all the other servants will snigger at you.
Yes, I have learned hard lessons,
And to you I may sound cynical and depressed.
But these hard lessons have taught me goodness.
Now each day, each week, each month, each year,
I seek to woo my wife.
She has been given to me by the gods of love,
So the gods smile when she submits.

A God and a Goddess

Tonight we shall discover each other anew, dear wife.
Let us stand before each other in silence.
Let each in turn take off a garment,
And as each garment falls silently to the ground
Let us pause and stare at each other,
Enjoying the part of the body newly revealed.
When we are both naked we shall stand still;
Motionless, we shall fill our eyes with each other.
In my eyes you shall be a goddess:
What others may regard as imperfections
Will to me be signs of your divinity.
And in your eyes make me a god:
Let my flabbiness become firm,
And my weakness become strength.
Once we have made each other divine

Let us lie down face to face.
Clasping one another firmly and intertwining our legs
We shall kiss each other deeply.
The nipples of our breasts will be pressed together,
And in body and soul we shall be as one.
You a goddess and I a god shall be united,
And the sky itself will tremble with joy.

Swapping Clothes

Once we took each other's garments.
I dressed like a woman in your clothes,
You dressed like a man in mine.
We had grown bored with each other.
We had lost interest in each other.
So by wearing each other's garments
We looked at each other with new eyes.
You were so handsome and I so pretty;
I wanted you as a man.
You wanted me as a woman.
Like gods creating all living things
To please their eyes,
So we re-created each other
To please our eyes.

To a Prostitute

Each week tens, even hundreds of men come to you.
In their hour of love they imagine themselves
To be the only one for whom you really care.

You are a brilliant actress, a superb dissembler.
You make each man seem special.
In your arms each man feels like a prince,
With you as his beloved princess.
At the end of the hour, as the dream fades,
They pay you gold and disappear;
And then you receive another deluded prince.
Are you a good woman, or are you evil?
Are you giving a valuable service
To men who in their hearts are lonely and miserable?
Or are you a destroyer of virtue,
A woman who causes men to stray
From the path of marital fidelity?
Once when I too was lonely and miserable,
When I could feel no love for my wife,
I became your prince, and you my princess.
You brought me back to life again,
You gave me strength to enjoy my lot.
Yet my contempt for my wife grew deeper,
My soul was caught between joy and bitterness.
You are both an agent of God
And an agent of evil.

CATULLUS

The greatest lyric poet of ancient Rome, his most famous love poem is also a hymn to Hymen, the god of lovers. The other Roman gods of love, Venus and Cupid, also frequently appear in his verses. He died in 54 BC aged only thirty.

To Hymen, God of Lovers

Garland your hair with marjoram,
Put a veil, sprayed with scent, over your face,
And saffron shoes on your milk-white feet.
On your wedding day we serenade you
With songs of love and joyful lust.
We dance in your honour,
Holding high a flaming torch.
His penis will burn like that torch,
And you shall delight in his heat.
You are blessed by the gods,
And heaven rejoices in your joy.
They fashioned you with special care
As if you were a statue in a temple.

Indeed your husband will worship you
As the goddess of his heart.
So as ivy twines close to a tree,
Twine your body with his body,
Twine your heart with his heart.

O Hymen, forerunner of Venus,
Master of the wedding-day,
Lord of the wedding-night,
You are the god of lovers.
The bride, laying aside her girlhood,
Awaits your footsteps.
The eager groom, discovering his manhood,
Can hardly contain his excitement.
Hymen, you will pluck the girl
Like a flower from her mother's arms,
And lay her in his manly arms.
Without your aid there is no love,
And thus no joy in a bodily union.
You make his manhoood rise
And her womanhood moist,
Thus enabling them to celebrate their bond.

Open the doors; the bride is here.
The wedding-torches shake their fiery heads
As the arms that carry them wave.
The shy young bride,
Half bashful and half excited,
Hesitates as she enters the throng.
Hymen, O Hymen, you bless this day.

This ordinary girl becomes a goddess,
This ordinary man a god.
The torches now bow their heads
To honour her virginal beauty.
A few short years ago they were children
Playing games in the orchard.
Their laughter was innocent and free of care.
Now they confront one another as man and woman.
Their childhood laughter is now adult desire.
The marriage-bed, with its polished legs,
Beckons them to take their pleasure.
From the adult youth of today
To the childish senility of old age
These two are bound in love.
Hymen, O Hymen, let their love
Be a constant source of pleasure.

Come, handsome young man,
And take your bride.
Venus is with you; step forward.
Your love for her is manifest to all.
It would be easier to count the grains of sand
In the infinite desert of Africa
Than to count the games of love
You two will play.
Only mature adults can play love's games;
Yet love's games make adults into children.
In the ecstasy of the marriage bed
The inhibitions of adulthood are thrown off,
The shackles of convention abandoned,

And husband and wife discover a new purity,
The innocence of loving sexual pleasure.
Hasten the marriage ceremony,
Let the knot be tied.
Then we shall slip away and close the door.
The night belongs to you,
And to Hymen, the god of love.

Cupid's Sneeze

Acme lay in Septimus' lap.
'Acme, perfection made flesh,'
He said, stroking her hips;
'I'm your abject slave.
I want nothing more
Than to love and serve you.
The only reward I ask
Is the gift of your love.'
And as he spoke,
Cupid sneezed twice,
On her and on him.
Then Acme, looking up at him,
Stared into his eyes
Which were watery with love,
And she touched his lips
Which were bruised with kisses.
'My dearest Septimus,
My life, my love, my all,'
She replied, smiling gently;
'Let us both be slaves

To the god of love.
My breast burns like a furnace,
My body is hot with desire.
Only by submitting to love
Can I find coolness and peace.'
And as she spoke, Cupid sneezed twice,
On her and on him.

Surely we can all know such happiness.
Venus, smile upon everyone,
That all may be slaves to love.

The Sparrow

Little sparrow, you are my darling's darling.
She plays with you, holds you in her lap.
She feeds you from her hand.
She lets you peck at her breast.
She gives you the love
I wish she would give to me.
She allows you to make free with her,
And yet gives no glance to me.
Sparrow, little sparrow, tell me your secret.
How did you enter her zone of love?

God of love, god of desire,
Venus, Hymen, join the dirge.
Death has struck my darling's darling.
The little sparrow has died in her lap.
He used to sing for her, jump for her,

But now he is silent and still.
You shades of Hell,
You take all into your depths,
Even the most innocent, the most graceful.
You have murdered that sparrow,
And now my love is overwhelmed with grief,
Her eyes are red, her skin is puffy.

From death comes life, from grief comes love.
I have now become her sparrow.
With my beak I kiss her lips.
With my wing I caress her breasts.
She feeds me with her body.
Dear love, will I ever be sated?
Will my passion ever be exhausted?
Let me make love now,
And then make love again,
A hundred times, a thousand times,
And a thousand more, we shall love.
Venus has blessed us,
Cupid has enslaved us,
Hymen has strengthened us.
We shall lose count of our times of love.
No one can tax us for loving.

OVID

During his younger years he was acclaimed as the finest poet in Rome, enjoying universal favour. But in 8 AD, at the age of fifty, the emperor banished him to a remote town on the Black Sea. This exile came shortly after the publication of *The Art of Love*, his long erotic poem; and it seems the emperor disapproved of this work, and also regarded the poet as an accomplice in his granddaughter's adultery. The core of the poem is guidance to young men in the art of winning a woman's love.

Taming the Wild Beast

The art of love must be carefully learned
Like sailing, rowing, or driving a chariot.
Thanks to Venus, I am a Master,
An expert in the mysterious art of love.
Love is like a wild bull or a horse.
With skill a man can tame a bull
So it carries the yoke and pulls the plough.
With artistry a wild horse will yield
To the bit, the bridle and the rider.

Yet both bull and horse retain their strength,
And happily accept their master's command.
Love too must learn to pull a plough:
The plough is the woman's natural lust
Which must cut through the soil, her stubborn pride.
The body and spirit must willingly submit
To the disciplines of wooing and winning.

The Hunter and Angler

You are a raw recruit, a fresh young soldier,
New and untried in the battlefield of love.
Take your time, do not hurry,
Not every pretty girl is right for you.
Your youthful eyes are far bigger than your heart.
Of all the girls who take your fancy,
Only a tiny few could capture your heart.
So play the field, talk and flirt,
Expect little, but hope for much.
You are like a hunter catching a stag:
The skilful hunter knows where to spread his net.
You are like a fisherman catching trout:
The skilful angler knows where to cast his line.
Be cautious and watchful, studying girls
As hunter and angler study their prey.
Observe how they respond to your advances.
Those who come forward too quickly,
Flashing their eyes and baring their teeth,
Will take what love they want, and then
Leave you alone, heartbroken and miserable.

Those who give no flicker of a smile,
Whose eyes remain dull and lifeless,
Will prove reluctant, frigid lovers.
Your eyes may feast on the young and nubile,
Their complexions bright, their flesh firm,
But their characters are changing and unstable.
What you love now will soon melt away
Like mist on a summer's morning.
So focus on those with maturity,
Whose wants and interests are firmly fixed.
Admire those whose manners are modest,
And yet whose bodies burn with desire.
They will not overwhelm you, nor leave you,
But will be faithful and true in their love.
And in the practice of physical pleasure
You shall enjoy years of infinite variety.

Seduction by Politeness

Be cautious, but do not dither.
Look at many, but then choose one.
And once you have made your decision,
Act with courage, cunning and charm.
Do not reveal the full force of your feelings,
But show only a casual interest.
Ask her to come for a meal,
As if your only concern was her pleasure.
And when she comes be polite and considerate,
Yet do not overwhelm her with attention.
Pretend that you see some dust fall on her blouse,

And gently and carefully brush it off.
The touch of your hand will make her tremble,
But you will have shown none of your desire.
If her dress hangs low, dragging the ground,
Lean across and lift it as she walks,
Apologizing for the dirt on your floor.
She will shiver with delight at your action,
As she feels your body close to hers,
But you will have shown only good manners.
When she is about to sit on a chair,
Bend forward to adjust the cushion,
Letting your arm brush against her dress.
In these and so many subtle ways
You break down her female defences,
Without ever seeming to attack.
You are seducing her with good manners.
You are firing Cupid's arrows at her,
And she cannot even see the bow.

Uncloaking Convention

It is a convention hallowed by centuries of time
That man pursues and woman is pursued.
Yet the body and the heart of a woman
Are as forceful and as deep in their desire
As the body and the heart of a man.
So when the woman seems awkward and coy
Do not imagine her cold and unfeeling.
Rather she is playing the ancient game
Of reluctant lover, of modest bride.

Your weapon against such pretence
Is to be nonchalant, light, yet bold.
If she dons the cloak of modesty
Then you don the cloak of good manners.
The challenge is to undo her cloak
Before your own falls to the ground.
At each meeting find apparent reason
For your body and face to move close to hers.
Let the river of lust flow through her body,
Forcing her to giggle and to wiggle,
While you remain firmly in control.
If she is carried through the streets on a litter,
Walk by her side, talking amiably.
If she loiters on foot amidst colonnades and porches,
Dawdle beside her, smiling and chatting,
But on no account give your purpose away.
Admire from a distance the curve of her body,
Allow your desire to rise when you are out of sight.
But when you are close beside her, be cool and casual,
For by controlled courage you'll win the war.

The Moment of Truth

Once you are sure your scheme is succeeding,
Once you see she enjoys your closeness,
Then choose an evening to reveal your love.
This will be the night of the final strike.
Invite her to a place of peace and beauty,
A seat by a river, under the shade of a tree.
Bring to that place the finest of wines,

Two goblets of silver, and a plate of sweets.
Let your toga be white, without spot and dirt,
And spray it with perfume, sharp and tangy.
Let your sandals shine, and your hair be short,
And your teeth gleam like the oyster's pearl.
When she arrives, ask her to sit,
And talk about the birds and the plants around you.
Then move closer, so your hips touch.
Take her hand in yours, and rest them in her lap.
Pause for a moment, as if shy and diffident,
And in quiet, modest tones confess your love.
Do not expect any words in reply,
But seek her answer by stealing a kiss.
If her head turns to you, and she gives her lips,
You know for certain her heart is won.
If she fails to respond, and turns away,
Do not despair, but turn away too.
Let your breathing quicken, as if close to tears,
So compassion will melt her hard, stubborn heart.
After a few long minutes look back towards her,
And if she gazes at you with watery eyes,
Move again to kiss her, and she will submit.

The First Night of Love

When both have confessed their deepest love,
A different battle must be fought.
Yet in this battle neither must win,
But both man and woman should emerge as victors.
Both should feel the fullest pleasures of love,

Both be equal in their sublime joy.
Begin with low murmurs and soft kisses.
Express your desire in inarticulate groans.
Undress your beloved, garment by garment.
As each part of the body is revealed
Feast your eyes on its grace and beauty.
And let her undress you, garment by garment,
That she may enjoy your lithe physique.
Now quietly lead her to your bed of love
And let her lie down, her head on a pillow,
Yet with her slender legs dangling over the edge.
Stand or kneel beside her, caressing and kissing her,
Gently exploring every part of her naked body.
Slowly yet surely her desire will grow
Until finally it is she who pulls you upon her.
Even now remain gentle, cautious and calm.
Let her desire take the lead, for you to follow.
In this way the pleasure is prolonged
And both you and she will be fully satisfied.
As you feel the climax rising within you,
Speak out so she too may release herself.
Thus your joy will enhance hers, and her joy yours.
So you will lift one another to heaven itself.

Heavenly Joy

We hear of the gods drinking heavenly wine,
Or gorging themselves on delicious food.
Yet even amongst the greatest gods and goddesses
There is one pleasure above every pleasure.

It is the pleasure of love, the joy of union.
Love is the delight of heaven itself.
So when a man and a woman unite their bodies
They become divine, and their bed is heaven.
The first night of love is the first of many.
They can love a hundred, a thousand, a million times,
And the joy grows fuller, higher, deeper.
Their heaven, once opened, need never close.
Let them learn variety, acquire artistry.
Let each night of love have a different shape.
Let her sometimes play the man, and he the woman.
Let them sometimes be dogs or lions in the act of love.
Let imagination run riot in their bodily battle.
Then truly he will be a god, and she a goddess,
For the pleasure of love will last for ever.
But let me finish with a word of warning.
You desire to be gods, but your bodies are human.
Your stomach may have lines, your breasts may sag,
Your buttocks may be wrinkled, your chin double.
For humans to be gods, there must be illusion.
In the light of day, show only that which is perfect.
If your buttocks are poor, but your breasts are firm,
Then in daylight show only your naked front.
Your ugly parts must be reserved for nightfall.
Moreover, while gods are sleepless, needing no rest,
Humans can be drained by excessive love.
So like an athlete keep your body strong and supple,
And like a baby have ample sleep and rest.
Then Jupiter himself will admire your prowess.

JUDAISM

INTRODUCTION: JUDAISM

In the various religious cults which jostled with Judaism in ancient times the snake was commonly regarded as a phallic symbol, credited with having taught the first man and woman how to enjoy sexual intercourse. The serpent who spoke to Adam and Eve, in the Hebrew creation story recounted in the Book of Genesis, persuaded them that by eating from the tree of knowledge 'your eyes shall be opened, you shall be as gods, knowing good and evil'. The immediate consequences were disastrous. Adam and Eve were filled with shame at their own nakedness, and were expelled from the Garden of Eden. But, as the serpent had promised, they were now free to make their own judgements about right and wrong. And Adam had intercourse with Eve, who bore him two sons – and so they obeyed God's original command to 'be fruitful and multiply'.

This ambivalence in the Hebrew creation myth exemplifies the Jewish attitude to human sexuality. The Jewish Bible – the Old Testament, as Christians call it – is stuffed with regulations about sex. There are long lists of who is allowed to marry whom, and thus the degrees of affinity which count as incest. Punishments are prescribed for intercourse during menstruation. Adultery, homosexuality and transvestism are capital offences. And the precise sexual obligations of husband and wife towards one another are laid down. Taken as a whole the ancient Jewish law reflects deep anxiety about sex.

Yet their Bible rejoices in the joy of sexual love, regarding celibacy as unnatural and even sinful. The Book of Deuteronomy pronounces that 'when a man takes a new wife, he shall not go out with the army, nor shall he be charged with any business. He shall be at home for one year, to enjoy his wife'. And it contains in the Song of Songs one of the most beautiful love poems ever composed. Its erotic language has worried Jewish and Christian commentators alike, many of whom have interpreted it purely as a spiritual allegory of the individual's love for God. But to the ancient Hebrews it was a celebration of sexual passion, and its place within the canon of Scripture was asserted in the conviction that passion between a man and a woman in love is the supreme divine gift. As Rabbi Akiba said, 'the whole world was not worthy of the day it was given to Israel; all the Scriptures are holy, but the Song of Songs is holy of holies'.

The later books of the Jewish Bible – the so-called Wisdom Books – contain a number of poems about divine wisdom, which is regarded as the feminine principle of the universe. These poems at times express the devotion of a lover towards his beloved. The theme is developed in the Kabbalah, a long mystical treatise composed by Jews in

Spain in the medieval period. The universe is seen as ruled by two principles, male and female; and human fulfilment consists in unifying these two principles both within the soul and through sexual union.

SONG OF SONGS

Written in the fifth century BC, it takes the form of a dialogue between a man and a woman, extolling their love. Both Jews and Christians regard it as part of their Scriptures, but have been troubled by it, both because of its overt eroticism, and because it makes no mention of God. Many have tried to interpret it as an allegory of the divine love between God and the soul. But most scholars today believe it should be taken literally as a beautiful love poem; and its honoured place in the Bible shows that God blesses sexual love.

THE WOMAN

May your lips cover me with kisses.
Your love is better than wine;
Your name itself is like fragrant oil.
No woman could help loving you.
Be my king and take me to your room;
Let us enjoy one another, losing ourselves in love.

THE MAN

My love, you excite me
As a mare excites the stallions of Pharaoh's chariots.
Your hair is beautiful on your cheeks,
And falls upon your neck like jewels.

THE WOMAN

While my king lies upon his couch,
My perfume fills the air with its fragrance.
My beloved has the scent of myrrh
As he lies upon my breasts.
He is like the wild flowers
That bloom in the vineyards of Egypt.

THE MAN

How beautiful you are, my love;
Your eyes shine with desire.

THE WOMAN

How handsome you are, my beloved.
The green grass will be our bed.
The cedar branches will be the beams of our house
And the cypress trees our roof.
I am a rose of Sharon,
A lily of the valleys.

THE MAN

As a rose among thorns
Is my love among women.

THE WOMAN

As an apple tree in the forest
Is my beloved among men.
I sit beneath his shadow
And taste his sweet, ripe fruit.
I am weak with passion.
His left hand is under my head,
And his right hand caresses me.

THE MAN

Arise, my love. Come with me.
The winter is over and the rains have gone.
Flowers rise from the earth.
Doves sing in the fields.
Figs are beginning to ripen
And the vines are in blossom,
Filling the air with their fragrance.
You are like a dove hiding in the cleft of a rock.
Let me see your beautiful face
And hear your enchanting voice.

THE WOMAN

My beloved is mine, and I am his.
Asleep in my bed, night after night,
I dreamt of the one I love.
I looked for him, but could not find him.
I wandered through the city, along its streets and alleys,
Looking for the one I love.
I looked, but could not find him.
Then at last I saw him.
I held him, and would not let him go.
I took him to my mother's house,
To the room where I was born.

THE MAN

How beautiful you are, my love.
Your eyes shine with desire behind your veil.
Your hair dances like a flock of goats
Bounding down the hills of Gilead.
Your teeth are as white as sheep
That have just been shorn and washed.
Your lips are like a scarlet ribbon;
How lovely they are when you speak.
Your cheeks are like two halves of a pomegranate,
Your neck is like the tower of David,
Round and smooth.
Your breasts are like two fawns,
Twin deer feeding among lilies.
How sweet is your love, dear bride,

It is sweeter than wine
And more fragrant than any perfume.
Your lips taste of honey
And your tongue of milk.
You are like a secret garden
Where the sweetest fruit and the finest spices grow.
Water gushes from a fountain and flows through you
Like a stream gushing down Mount Lebanon.

THE WOMAN

Awake, north wind. Come, south wind.
Blow in my garden and fill the air with fragrance.
Let my beloved come to his garden
And eat its choicest fruits.

THE MAN

I have entered my garden, my love.
I am gathering spices and myrrh.
I am eating honey and drinking wine.

THE WOMAN

While I sleep, my heart is awake.
I dream that my beloved knocks at the door.

THE MAN

Let me come in, my darling, my love.
My head is wet with dew
And my hair damp from the mist.

THE WOMAN

I have already undressed;
Why should I dress again?
I have washed my feet;
Why should I soil them again?
My beloved puts his hand to the latch,
And my heart leaps within me.
I open the door for him.
My beloved is handsome and strong,
His face is bronzed and smooth.
His hair is wavy, and black as a raven.
His eyes are like doves washed in milk.
His cheeks are like beds of fragrant spices.
His lips are like lilies wet with myrrh.
His body is like smooth ivory.
His thighs are like columns of alabaster.
He is majestic, like the mountains of Lebanon.
His mouth is sweet to kiss.
He is mine, and I am his.

THE MAN AND THE WOMAN

Let us drink the wine of passion
Until we are drunk with love.

WISDOM BOOKS

In the centuries immediately preceding Christ the main theme of Jewish literature was the acquisition of wisdom. Collections of wise proverbs were made, addressed particularly to young men; and philosophical books were written reflecting on the inner purpose of life. In addition poems were written in praise of wisdom, which was personified as a beautiful woman emanating from God. Sometimes the poems were composed as if by Wisdom herself, and sometimes as if by one of her lovers.

Wisdom Speaks Her Own Praises

I came forth from the mouth of God,
And I covered the earth like mist.
I had my tent on the highest mountain
And my throne on a pillar of cloud.
I strode across the dome of the sky
And I walked along the bottom of the sea.
I held sway over every people and nation,
Over the waves of the sea and the whole earth.
At the beginning of eternity God created me,

And for all eternity I shall remain.
I am as tall as a cedar on Mount Lebanon,
As elegant as a cypress on Mount Hermon.
I am as slender as a palm in Engedi,
As beautiful as a rose in Jericho.
I am as fragrant as perfume of cinnamon,
As tantalizing as the scent of acacia.
My limbs are as gracious as terebinth branches,
As supple as the shoots of the vine.
Come to me, all who desire me,
And take your fill of my fruits.
Loving me is sweeter than honey,
Possessing me brings joy for ever.
Those who eat me hunger for more.
Those who drink me thirst for more.

In Love with Wisdom

She is the breath of God's power,
The pure emanation of God's glory.
Nothing impure can enter her.
She is a reflection of the eternal light,
The untarnished mirror of God's grace,
The image of his holiness.

Although she is alone, she can do everything.
Herself unchanging, she makes all things new.
In each generation she enters men's souls
To make them into lovers of God.
God loves only those whom she has entered.

She is more splendid than the sun.
She outshines all the constellations.
She is brighter than light itself.

From my youth I have loved her.
From my earliest years I have searched for her.
I resolved to make her my bride.
I fell in love with her beauty.
Her closeness to God made her a princess to me.
If in this life we should desire wealth,
She is worth more than gold or silver.
If in this life we should desire knowledge,
She can teach me all there is to know.
If in this life we should desire virtue,
She can show me the ways of virtue.

So I have decided to share my life with her.
She shall be my partner in times of prosperity and peace,
And my comfort in times of anxiety and sadness.
Through her, immortality shall be mine.

KABBALAH

A collection of mystical writings by Jews living in Spain in the medieval period, much of it is incomprehensible to the ordinary reader. But two short passages on sexuality express clearly that Jewish mystics, unlike their Christian counterparts in the same periood, regarded sexual pleasure as a divine gift which can deepen our understanding of God.

Male and Female

When is a person in union?
A person is in union when the male and the female principle
Within the soul are in union.
A person is in union when he or she is united
With a member of the opposite sex.
The man and the woman should have a single desire
For union within themselves.
Then the hour of union between themselves
Shall give them perfect joy.
At that time there shall be perfect unity
Of both body and soul.

They shall form one body,
And the male and the female principle
Shall form one soul.
When male and female are in union
God abides.

Divine Sexual Unity

When souls descend into the world they separate into masculine and feminine forms. This brings disunity on earth. The man has to assert his masculinity, becoming aggressive and dominant. The woman has to assert her femininity, becoming gentle and submissive. Thus men fight one another, while women are helpless to bring peace. And men want to treat women as slaves, while the women feel bitter and resentful at their own weakness.

But sexual arousal is the means by which unity can be restored. The man desires the woman for herself. If he merely demands sexual intercourse, without her consent, he will get no satisfaction, since she will remain inert and unresponsive under him. So he must gently woo her and love her. The woman for her part desires the man for himself. If she remains wholly submissive, she too will get no satisfaction. So in the heat of passion she must assert herself, playing an equal part in the act of union.

Thus sexual intercourse is a great spiritual teacher. Satisfaction is only achieved if the man discovers the female principle within himself, and the woman discovers the male principle within herself. In sexual union the divine unity of heaven is restored.

Sexual Meditation

Imagine yourself sitting between two thrones. Each throne is bathed in light. Look at each throne in turn. They are both made of gold, and are studded with jewels of every colour.

At first the thrones are empty. Then on one throne a man appears. He is young, handsome and strong, dressed in the finest robes. And on the other throne a woman appears. She is young, beautiful and slender, dressed in the finest robes. The man and the woman seem to be looking towards you, but you realize they are looking across you to each other. In their eyes you can see passionate desire: each wants the other.

But they do not move from their thrones. Their desire for each other passes right through you, and you feel it as your own. You desire her with the same passion as he does. You desire him with the same passion that she does. Your whole body trembles with desire.

Now you begin to feel heat on either side of your body. The two thrones are slowly moving towards you. As they draw closer the heat grows stronger until it is so intense you can hardly bear it. Finally the two thrones meet within your body. A surge of pleasure runs through you and you lie back exhausted.

In that moment you have discovered yourself and discovered heaven.

CHRISTIANITY

INTRODUCTION: CHRISTIANITY

Although the New Testament is silent on the subject, Jesus is normally assumed to have been celibate; and he himself exalted those who became 'eunuchs for the kingdom of God'. His only sexual teaching was to demand the strictest fidelity between husband and wife, condemning even men who 'commit adultery in the heart' by 'looking on another woman with lust'. Yet, despite his elevated morality, he shocked his contemporaries by mixing with prostitutes and by defending a woman caught in adultery; as he asserted, he was called to save 'not respectable people, but outcasts and sinners'.

Paul, the main interpreter of the new faith, was proud of his own celibacy, believing it conferred greater spiritual zeal and energy; and he urged those with sufficient self-discipline to follow his example. He was not concerned with procreation since he believed that the end of the universe would be soon; so the only purpose of marriage was 'as a remedy against fornication': in his oft-quoted phrase 'it is better to marry than to burn with passion'.

Thus from the start celibacy was regarded as the sexual ideal. And when the monastic movement began in the third century, with hundreds and thousands of men and women retreating into the deserts and forests to live as hermits and in small communities, the cult of celibacy was reinforced. By the eleventh century the Pope was insisting that all priests should be celibate, and this remains the rule in the Roman Catholic Church. Naturally the majority of Christians continued to marry, and there are numerous stories of priests, monks and nuns breaking their vows. But sex was regarded as at best a necessary evil – or even, in the teaching of St Augustine, the means by which the sin of Adam and Eve is passed from one generation to another. As a result Christianity is alone amongst the major religions in having no sex manuals; on the contrary, in medieval times priests were issued with lists of penances for people who confessed to any kind of sexual activity beyond that necessary for procreation. Even rear entry was banned as this was deemed to augment the pleasure of intercourse.

Yet if physical sex is frowned upon, sexual feelings themselves remain irrepressible. Thus Christianity is the richest of all religions in erotic writing addressed to God. The works of the great Christian mystics, such as Teresa of Avila and John of the Cross, overflow with sexual imagery, often of the most explicit kind. At first this may seem shocking, even perverted. But the level of spiritual ecstasy which these mystics attained suggests that the human sexual instinct can find fulfilment by spiritual, as well as physical, means.

One of the most famous, and tragic, love stories in all history is that of Abelard and Héloïse. These brilliant and impetuous lovers were forced to separate, and live in monasteries. Their letters, which must move even the most unromantic heart, are a testimony to both the agony and the peace of celibate sexuality.

JORDAN OF SAXONY

In 1221 he was elected leader of the Order of Preachers, on the death of its founder St Dominic. By all accounts he was a sweet-natured and charming man, who attracted numerous female admirers. A year after his election he travelled to Bologna where he encountered a beautiful, aristocratic young nun, Diana. Over the following decade and a half they corresponded regularly, sharing their most intimate feelings. Sadly only his letters to her survive. He never condemns her youthful passion, but tries to direct it towards God. The popular image of the nun as Christ's bride constantly recurs.

Before Her Spiritual Wedding

You write to me of your desire, both spiritual and physical, for Christ; and you feel confused and anxious about the intensity of that desire. Your confusion arises from a natural fear. You are betrothed to Christ; you know that in a few months' time you shall be his bride. The desire you feel is the same as a young girl feels towards the man she is to marry. But such a girl also feels fear, as you do. She is worried about whether she will make a good wife; and she is frightened of the intimacy of marriage. Similarly you are worried as to whether you will be able to serve Christ as your spiritual husband; and you do not yet know what intimacy with him really involves.

It is no use trying to overcome your fear. What matters now is that you prepare yourself to be Christ's bride. Do not attempt any extra prayer, as you are probably too nervous to sit in silent meditation for any length of time. Follow the example of the bee, gathering honey from the flowers of the earth, to store up as food for the future. You can gather spiritual food through extra acts of charity towards your sisters in the convent. Find new ways of helping and serving them. Each virtuous act will be like spiritual honey that will add extra sweetness to your marriage to Christ.

After Her Spiritual Wedding

You have rejected the wealth and the vanities of the world, and taken Jesus Christ as your bridegroom: for his sake you have chosen poverty. Yet is it really poverty you have chosen? Rather it is poverty you have rejected, and chosen riches – the riches of Christ's marvellous kingdom. Indeed you are not just a bride but a queen, because you are married to the King, and enjoy all the sumptuous wealth of his court.

The wedding-feast itself was the promise of what is to come. When you made your vows – when you gave up the material and physical pleasures of the world – the angels in heaven broke into joyful song. And at that moment the bread and the wine of his body and blood became for you the nuptial banquet.

Yet, in the most wonderful miracle of all, the banquet is also the consummation of the marriage. Your bridegroom comes to you dressed in robes of gold, his face shining with love. You come before him in white robes of purity, your face bowed in humility. Then he gives you his body. What joy! What rapture! The King of heaven and earth has actually made himself yours that you might belong to him.

Those vows of poverty and chastity are your marriage vows. In the eyes of the world they imply sacrifice and deprivation. And certainly all of us who have lived under these vows do at times feel the lack of worldly wealth and pleasure. But if only the world could see the true wealth and the true pleasure which we enjoy!

The Dullness of Marriage

Your letter is full of anxiety. You are anxious about changes being made in your convent. You are anxious about your physical health. You are anxious about the sisters whom you especially love. You are carrying a great load of anxiety on your heart.

Have you forgotten who is your husband; have you forgotten who is looking after you, cherishing you, caring for your every need? There is no need for this anxiety. You have every reason to be confident and joyful, free from all worries. He will ensure that the changes which those in authority are making in your convent are wholesome and

176

good. He will give you health or sickness as you need it for your own spiritual well-being. And your sisters are also brides of Christ, just as you are, so he is cherishing them also.

But I know that these words of reassurance will not reach your heart. The first youthful pleasure and zest in being wedded to Christ has gone, and now the marriage seems dull and dreary by comparison. It is not that you want to break your vows of poverty and chastity: you do not want an earthly husband with earthly riches. But even a heavenly marriage to the King of kings can lose its sparkle, and the acts of love can seem empty and meaningless.

Do not despair. None of us deserves joy or pleasure; in truth we deserve only misery and pain. Jesus did not have to take you as his bride; if he had judged you on your spiritual merits, he would have made you a lowly slave. Any pleasure which comes from our relationship with him is a gift, not a right. When you first made your vows, he showered gifts upon you. And you naturally thought that marriage to Christ would always be as blissful as in those early days. But now he is testing your faithfulness. He is asking you to remain loyal to him even when you gain nothing from it.

In fact he is no longer treating you as a young girl, but as a mature woman who can be trusted. Do not regard your current state as a sign of his rejection. On the contrary, it is a sign of his respect.

Jealous Warnings

Words spoken by a friend of the bridegroom may be very different from those spoken by the bridegroom himself. So I know that what I want to write to you is weak and empty compared with your direct communication with Christ.

But I am jealous on the bridegroom's behalf, and I feel compelled to express my jealousy. Yes, you have remained faithful to him during this long period of dullness and dryness in your marriage. Yet you have started to punish yourself in ways which cannot be pleasing to him. Instead of simply fasting in the ways and at the times prescribed by your convent's rule, you are fasting continuously, depriving yourself of the food and drink necessary for your health. You are going without rest and sleep, rising out of bed through the cold hours of the night to pray. But are you really praying, or just shivering?

You imagine yourself pious and virtuous; but there is no piety in such excess. In punishing yourself you are punishing him who loves you. In your heart you are angry and resentful that he no longer treats you like a young bride, and you are expressing your anger by destroying yourself. You imagine that he will take pity on you, and once again shower gifts of joy and pleasure on you, in order to save you from this excess. Certainly he is full of compassion for you, and longs for you to care for yourself as he cares for you. But how can he submit to this childish anger? If he were to respond to your wishes, he would be turning himself from a King into a slave, at your beck and call.

I beg you to return to your senses. Eat what you are offered, no more and no less. Rest at the times which are given for rest, and pray at the times given for prayer. And be patient. If you will wait calmly and quietly, he will – when you are spiritually ready – come to you with gifts of joy that are beyond all dreams.

Mature Pleasures

I am delighted that you have thrown away the false flowers of self-inflicted suffering, and are now regaining the true flowers of virtue. You are eating and resting properly, so you have the energy to work hard for your sisters. Yes, there is indeed special satisfaction in caring for the old and the sick.

And I am doubly delighted that your bridegroom is once again revealing to you his love – and, as I had promised, showering upon you new and greater joys. I do not fully understand the mind of Christ, but I believe it is those flowers of virtue that have drawn him back to you. Those are the flowers which adorn the bridal chamber and are strewn over the nuptial bed. To him nothing is more enticing than the flowers of virtue. Charity, humility, meekness, gentleness, generosity – those are plucked from the garden of heaven, to win the heart of the King of heaven.

I can tell from your letter that you feel again the excitement that you knew as a young bride. Yet there is also a new depth, a new fullness to your joy. In your heart there is a serenity and peace which are the fruits of faithfulness and loyalty. You no longer doubt yourself nor doubt his love, so you can submit yourself freely to his caresses. You have grown from young bride to mature wife, and discovered that, unlike an earthly marriage, a heavenly marriage gets better as the years pass!

RAMON LULL

The island of Majorca, where he was born in 1233, had been until a few years earlier under Islamic rule. While remaining a devout Christian, he was deeply influenced by Islamic mystical thought. And his most famous work, *The Book of the Lover and the Beloved*, is a fusion of Islam and Christianity. It is written in the form of short paragraphs, often apparently unconnected, which describe a love affair between a human soul and God.

Reflections of His Beauty

The Lover rose early and went to seek his Beloved. He found travellers in the road and asked if they had seen his Beloved. They were surprised, and replied, 'How did you lose sight of your Beloved?' 'Even when I cannot see my Beloved', the Lover said, 'there is a picture of him always in my mind, because his beauty is reflected in every living creature.'

The Doorway to Love

The keys of the door of love are gilded with sighs and tears. The door is fashioned from devotion and desire. The light which beckons on the other side is joy and satisfaction. The Lover beat upon the door with all his might. The Beloved heard the blows, and was glad, opening the door to the Lover. The Lover went in and embraced the Beloved.

Two Fires

There are two fires that burn within the Lover. One is made of pleasure and desire; the other of fear and grief. The Lover fears that he will never again see his Beloved, and is overwhelmed with grief. Yet the Lover never ceases to desire his Beloved, and when his Beloved appears his pleasure knows no bounds.

Loving and Love

The Lover asked his Beloved: 'Which is greater, loving or love itself?' The Beloved answered: 'Love is the tree; the joy of loving is the fruit of the tree, the leaves are the sorrows of loving. Yet when love is made perfect, the tree, its fruits and its leaves become one – so the joys and sorrows of loving are absorbed into love itself.

Embrace and Kiss

The Beloved revealed himself to the Lover, dressed in new robes of bright scarlet. The Beloved stretched out his arms to embrace the Lover, and bent down to kiss him. The embrace and the kiss lasted for ever.

Heart and Body

In the heart of the Lover the Beloved planted desire, and watered the seed with the tears of grief. In the body of the Lover the Beloved planted anguish, and watered the seed with tears of joy.

Home and Bed

The Beloved entered the home of the Lover, casting out all darkness, and filling it with the light of love. The Beloved blessed the bed of the Lover, and kissed his pillow, so at night the Lover would only dream of the Beloved.

Afflictions of Love

The Lover yearned for his Beloved, and sent him his thoughts, that the Beloved might send back his bliss. Instead the Beloved sent sighs and tears, saying that the bliss of love can only come after great trials and tribulations. So the Lover sang: 'Ah, what an affliction is love! What suffering the Beloved sends to his Lovers! Yet every pain which pierces his Lovers' hearts and bodies is a sign of infinite love.'

The Prison of Love

The Lover journeyed over hill and dale, seeking some way to escape the prison of love. He found a hermit sleeping beside a spring. He wakened the hermit to ask if in his dreams he had seen the Beloved. The hermit answered that, whether sleeping or waking, he was held captive in the prison of love. The Lover was overjoyed to find a fellow prisoner, and they both sat down and wept, their tears mingling with the water from the spring.

Piercing the Cloud

A dark cloud came between the Lover and the Beloved, so the Lover could no longer see his Beloved. The Beloved pierced the cloud with his body, embracing and kissing the Lover. And the Lover fainted with ecstatic joy.

The Bed of Love

The Beloved clothed the Lover in a soft crimson robe, and then laid him on a bed surrounded by white flowers. The Beloved lay beside the Lover, and the air filled with the sweetest song.

ABELARD AND HÉLOÏSE

In the twelfth century France seethed with theological controversy, and Peter Abelard was the country's most brilliant debater. An elderly priest, called Fulbert, entrusted Abelard with the education of his intelligent and beautiful daughter Héloïse. They fell in love and she became pregnant, so they secretly married. Fulbert was enraged and had Abelard emasculated, and he then sent his daughter to a convent. Heartbroken, Abelard entered a monastery. They continued to write to each other, and their passionate letters express their spiritual struggle as they try to channel their mutual desire towards God.

Abelard to Héloïse

I have a picture of you in my room: I never pass it without stooping to look at it. When we were together I barely glanced at it. But as each day passes that we are apart, the picture seems to become an ever more faithful likeness of you. My love for you brings this whole canvas, and the colours and lines upon it, to life. So, if a picture can give such pleasure, surely letters can inspire our lonely hearts.

Letters have a soul; they can speak; they contain all the fire of our passions; they can be as soft and as delicate as speech – and in their boldness of expression may even go beyond speech.

Let us write frequently to each other. Such an innocent pleasure surely cannot be forbidden us. Let us not lose through negligence the only pleasure that is left to us, the only joy which the malice of our enemies cannot snatch from us. In our letters we can truly be husband and wife. In spite of all our miseries, we can be what we please in letters. Having lost the pleasure of seeing and possessing you, I shall in some measure compensate this loss by embracing your letters. There I shall listen to your most secret thoughts; I shall carry them always with me, next to my heart; and in quiet moments I shall take them out and kiss them. If you remain capable of jealousy, be jealous for the fond caresses I bestow on your letters. Write to me spontaneously, without thinking in advance what you have to say: I want to read the words of your heart, not of your brain. I cannot live unless you tell me always that you love me.

Héloïse to Abelard

I have been called to the cloister not out of zeal or devotion, but by my love for you and my relations' condemnation of that love. Here I am, and here I will remain. I am not repentant about what has happened between us. I have not put on these robes of chastity because I want to abase myself before God. I am imprisoned in this place because of our disgrace in the eyes of others, whose judgement I reject. I live among those who are wedded to Christ, yet I am wedded to a man. Among those who are slaves to His cross, I am a slave to human passion. I am head of a religious community, yet I am devoted only to Abelard – to you.

May God bring light to my darkness. Is it his grace or my despair which compels me to write so honestly to you, dear Abelard? In this temple of chastity I am covered with the ashes of the fire which consumed us. I confess that I am a sinner; yet I weep not for my sins, but for you, my love. Far from abhorring my sins, I only add fuel to the fire. Far from being ashamed of the passion we shared, I want only to renew it.

Good God, in what a terrible mire of disorder you have plunged me! I know what obligations this veil places upon me, but I feel far more strongly the obligation of human passion. Sometimes I am swayed by sentiments of piety, and the next moment my entire heart and body are given over to amorous desires. In my will I have resolved to love you no more, and to be true to my present calling. Yet from the very depths of my being there rises up a surge of emotion which overwhelms my will and darkens my pious devotion. You reign in the innermost areas of my soul where I cannot attack you. When I try to break the chains which bind me to you, my attempts are mere self-deception.

I have renounced life, stripping myself of everything, but I cannot renounce you, my Abelard. I have lost my lover, but I still preserve my love. O vows! O convent! I have not abandoned my humanity under your stern discipline, but I have clasped my human passion to my breast with every ounce of my strength. You have not turned me into marble by changing my clothes. You have not hardened my heart by imprisoning me behind hard stone walls. Outwardly I obey your rules, but inwardly my soul itself rebels.

O Abelard, you alone can turn my human love into divine love. Let us together be wedded to Christ. Let the passion we possess for one another be turned towards him. Tell me how this divine love can be nourished. Show me how human love can be purified. Without changing the ardour of our affection, let us change its object. Let our songs of human love become hymns of divine love.

Abelard to Héloïse

I promise myself I will forget you, and yet I cannot think of you without loving you, and am pleased with the thought. My love is not at all weakened by those pious meditations I force myself to undertake in order to free myself from you. The silence which surrounds me is like an empty barn which my mind fills with my passion for you.

I hate you and I love you. I am ashamed of my love for you, which contradicts my calling. In my weakness I seek to support myself on the Cross of Christ. I know that I am serving two masters, divine love and human love, and am being torn apart. You can see in what utter confusion I find myself. Religion commands me to pursue virtue, since human love offers me no hope. But love still dominates my imagination, filling my head with memories of past pleasures. Piety is not always the fruit of retirement to the cloister; human passion can grow stronger amidst holy solitude. My passion grows furious by impotence; I am in a rage of love for you. I continually think of you. I continually call to mind that day when you first embraced me.

O Lord, if in this condition I run to church and lie prostrate before your altar, beseeching you to pity me, why do you not turn the fire of my passion into the pure flame of your Holy Spirit? Can you not look down on these monastic robes of penitence which I wear, and make my heart truly penitent?

You too, dear Héloïse, profane your vocation with your words of love. You too blaspheme, insulting God by wearing robes of righteousness over a heart and body filled with sin. I prayed that your feelings would change, and that this in time would cause my feelings to change. It is said that we die to the affection of those whom we see no more – that absence is the tomb of love. Yet in our case absence only increases the torment. I over-estimated my own virtue, convincing myself that once we were apart you would stay only in my memory, without troubling my mind. Héloïse, I am angry: angry with myself for loving you so passionately: angry with you for returning that love.

I have never been tempted by wealth or public praise; these things have always been nothing to me. Yet your charm, your beauty, the fragrant air that surrounds you, your moist eyes looking at me so tenderly, your gentle speech assuring me of your love – all these things have pierced my heart. And in spite of my fervent ambition to serve my God, I instead become slave of my passion for you. Yet you have now renounced the world, and I too have taken the vows of a monk. We each took our vows in the presence of God. Shall we now renounce them? Shall we now flee from God's love in order to indulge our love? I pass whole days and nights in this cloister without closing my eyes, consumed by the fiery flames of passion. What joys we have abandoned, what pleasures we now miss by our separation! O Héloïse, I should not say such things to you. I write love songs to you which then I burn, in the hope that my passion will be consumed by its own flames.

My whole body cries out for you to be here. I want you to thrust yourself between God and me, so my eyes can be filled with the true object of my love – which is you. Yet I hate myself and hate you for such desires. Forget me. Give yourself wholly to God. I shall rejoice in your holiness. Make yourself an example to all who aspire to virtue. Be assiduous in your worship, diligent in your spiritual reading, unselfish towards the nuns in your charge. Do not listen to my words of passion, but only to the instructions of those who are themselves holy and pious. Do not drink from the cup of human love, but only from the chalice of Christ's love. Look only on him, and never on me.

God's Church is jealous of its glory, and commands that her children serve only her. There can be no compromise, no deceit. She demands that I forget you, and that you forget me. We must return to God by turning away from one another. When God himself is our rival we have nothing to fear. If we devote ourselves to him alone, he will bring us the satisfaction we desire. He will console us. He will bring us pleasure that lasts for all eternity. Let us blush, let us weep for our past sins. Even while our hearts do not wholly belong to him, let us do everything in our power to give our hearts to him.

Dear Héloïse, we have taught each other how to love. Let that habit of love, learnt from one another, now be offered to Jesus Christ.

Héloïse to Abelard

At last, Abelard, you have lost Héloïse for ever. Despite my belief that you would always fill my heart and mind, I have now banished you from my thoughts. Once I thought that you as my lover were the only hope of happiness; once I thought your image would follow my every step, and be with me at my dying breath. Now I can forget you.

I confess without a blush that I am unfaithful to you, that my love for you has proved inconstant. Let my inconstancy teach the world that there is no virute in depending upon the passions of women. Does this trouble you, Abelard; does it surprise you? Did you ever imagine that Héloïse could be fickle? I loved you once so strongly that it must seem impossible that my love is now extinguished. But when I tell you what rival has taken my heart from you, you will surely praise me. It is God alone who has ravished me and seized me as his own. Yes,

Abelard, he gives that peace, that serenity which our human love never afforded. What other rival would ever have taken me from you? Could any mortal have blotted out my love for you? Could I be guilty of sacrificing the virtuous and learned Abelard to anyone other than God?

Let me tell you how God in his secret providence won the victory. A few days after receiving your last letter I fell dangerously ill. My condition was so bad the physicians told me to expect death within a week. As I lay on my bed of pain my passion for you, which in my heart I had always believed was pure and innocent, now seemed utterly criminal. Without effort my memory caused me to live, within my mind, my years on earth again. As I recalled my past, everything was happy and sweet except my love for you, which seemed painful and bitter. Death, which until then I had always considered at a distance, now presented itself to me as it appears to sinners. I began to dread the wrath of God. Those times of passion which we shared, those tender letters which we exchanged, now caused me as much pain as they had once caused pleasure. I was filled with remorse, and I prayed that I might be healed of the present illness, to have more time on earth to make amends. And God answered my prayer.

Solitude brings torment to a mind that is not at peace; its troubles increase in the midst of silence. Since I have been shut up in these walls, I have done nothing but weep for our misery; this cloister has echoed with my cries. Instead of fulfilling God's merciful plan for me, I have rebelled against him. I have looked upon this safe refuge like a prison. Instead of sanctifying myself by a life of penitence, I have indulged within myself my own sinful passions.

But now, Abelard, I have torn off that bandage which blinded me, and made myself truly worthy of your esteem. You are no longer the amorous Abelard who used incessantly to contrive new ways of deceiving our observers, and come to my room at night. Those happy moments of human pleasure are now to us both causes of horror. The soft and tender joys we shared are now bitter memories.

Yet I must be honest. Even as I write unwanted emotions arise within my breast. I have not fully triumphed over our love. In truth as long as I breathe I will in some measure sigh for you, dear Abelard. God has opened to me the full treasure of his mercy, and yet I cannot fully seize it. Perhaps I have exhausted his forgiveness. My passion is only a shadow of its former strength, so my sin and my need of mercy are much less than before my illness. Dear Abelard, pray for me! Dear God, do not now reject me!

Fear not, Abelard, I will not trouble you any further with my emotions. I will no more try to reawaken your own sinful passion for me. I will forget you as husband and lover, and look on you only as priest and father. I will ask nothing of you but spiritual advice. Where I once followed you in the ways of the flesh, I will now follow you in the ways of the Spirit. Please continue to write to me, confining yourself to matters of religion, so that I may learn to love you as God desires. And I will answer your letters at once, restricting myself also to religious things.

Abelard to Héloïse

Write no more to me, Héloïse, write no more; let us stop reminding ourselves of past pleasures. Such memories only disturb our souls, and render us incapable of relishing the sweet fruits of solitude. Let us mortify ourselves in body and mind, meditating only on God's love, and never again think of the human love that bound us.

Dear Héloïse, my deepest desire is to lift you up when you stumble, to strengthen you in your weakness, to enlighten you when your mind darkens, to comfort you when you are sad. Your heart still burns with that fatal fire which you cannot extinguish, and mine is torn apart by conflicting desires. For the last time, Héloïse, I shall open my heart to you. I have not yet broken the ties that bind me to you. I fight against my feelings of tenderness for you. I cannot read your letters without yearning to hold the hand that wrote them. I sigh, I weep; all my strength is not sufficient to hide my condition from those around me. This, unhappy Hèloïse, is the miserable condition of Abelard.

As you know, it was not from sincere repentance that I decided to retire from the world. But I now believe that the circumstances which drove us apart, and induced each of us to seek the refuge of the cloister, were the secret design of God. His will has been done despite me, not because of me. Both of us are now carrying the Cross of Christ on our shoulders; the weight which we feel from our past love is truly the weight of his redeeming love. Let us learn to bear his Cross without bitterness or resentment, but with grace and courage. Only then can we rise to new life with him.

Our Lord Jesus Christ is speaking to us. He is asking you to take him as your lover instead of me. Do not refuse such a husband. Listen to his soft, gentle voice. Allow your heart to beat faster in his presence, as it once beat faster in mine. Allow your body to yearn for his body, so that at each Communion, when you receive his body in the consecrated bread, your marriage to him will be consummated anew. Let each day in the cloister be a wedding day.

Farewell, Héloïse. These are the last words you will receive from Abelard. Heaven grant that your heart, once ruled by my love, be now ruled by Christ's love. May the image of your loving Abelard, always present in your mind, become an image of a penitent Abelard. And may we both shed as many tears for our salvation as we have shed for one another.

RICHARD ROLLE

He lived as a hermit on the Yorkshire moors, emerging every few months to walk from village to village singing the devotional songs he had composed. In an age when the organized religion of the Church had become formal and remote from ordinary people's concerns, his warm passionate verse had great appeal. He also wrote poems in a similar vein, which were widely circulated. He regarded his soul as a woman, seeking a divine bridegroom. He died of the Black Death in 1349.

Come Quickly

Lord Jesus, because of you I have rejected all earthly loves. I do not seek the love of man or woman. My heart desires neither wealth nor fame. Nothing in all creation can seduce me.

Remember how I turned away from sensual pleasures, how I shunned the charms of those who wanted me. Remember how I refused to indulge in rich food and fine wine.

I kept myself safe and pure for you, and you alone.

From the beginning you were the only object of my desire.

I have suffered much bodily pain. I have gone without food and drink in my search for you. I have endured bitter cold and sleepless nights as I have tried to find you.

My soul has pined for you, cried out for you. At times she has been on fire with longing for you. And at times she has been like dry ashes, in despair at your continued absence.

Come quickly, Lord Jesus. Satisfy my soul before she dies in misery. Give her a sign, a token of your love.

Take Pity

Jesus Christ, my Lord and God, take pity on me.

My soul is heavy with sorrow. My mind is utterly confused. My body is wasting away with sadness.

All that the world ever gave me I have given away. Nothing remains but my love for you. You are my only treasure.

If only you will come to me, I will work without wearying, rejoice without grieving, take pleasure without becoming sated.

Seeing you, loving you, praising you, I shall be satisfied for ever.

I Ask You

I ask you, Lord Jesus,
to nurture within me, your lover,
a desire for you that is unbounded,
an affection for you that is unchecked,
a longing for you that is unrestrained,
a fervour for you that throws discretion to the winds.
Let reason not hold back my passion.
Let fear not inhibit my passion.
Let judgement not hamper my passion.

Please Me with Your Love

My God, my Love, come upon me, pierce me with your love, wound me with your beauty. I long for your touch.

Pour your healing medicine into me, your faithful lover. My only desire is for you. My heart sinks for you, my soul pants for you, my body thirsts for you.

Yet you refuse to show yourself to me. You look away. You bar the door. You shun me. You even laugh at my anguish.

Why do you treat me like this? You have lifted me above all earthly desires. You have filled me with love for you. Why do you now refuse my love?

Come to me, Beloved. Let your love be like a dart, piercing my body. I have given up everything for you, my home, my wealth, my reputation.

Let me love you. Let me lie with you, and be at peace, my desire fulfilled.

The Knot of Love

No-one can untie the knot by which I am bound to you, Lord Jesus. We are joined together so firmly that no man can put us asunder.

Yet you refuse to satisfy me. You refuse to reveal yourself to me in all your beauty. You refuse to answer me when I cry for love.

I sing the sweetest songs for you. I speak constantly of my desire for you. I praise you in every word I utter.

Why do you remain so cold? Why do you treat your lover with such contempt? Are you trying to drive me away from you, into the arms of an earthly lover?

The Heat of Love

Jesus, when you are in me, and the heat of love is surging into me, I am on fire with joy.

I embrace you, I kiss you, I caress you. I hold nothing back. I submit my whole self to you.

Your beauty overwhelms me. My desire for you infuses my entire body, heart, mind and soul. I cry out with love.

When I turn away from love to eat and drink, you are in the food and wine I consume. When I fall asleep, you are in the dreams that fill my head.

TERESA OF AVILA

During her early years as a nun she suffered almost continual depressions. Then in 1555 at the age of forty she enjoyed a series of ecstatic spiritual experiences, which she interpreted as a mystical marriage to Christ. Her autobiography records with striking honesty her passionate emotions; and her poetic prayers are filled with erotic imagery. These experiences infused her with enormous energy, and over the following three decades she founded a new religious order with convents through-out her native Spain. Numerous portraits and sculptures of her in a state of ecstasy have been made.

Portrait of Christ

I found it so difficult to picture things in my mind that, if I could not actually see a thing, I had no mental picture of it. So, although I could think of Jesus Christ, I could not see him. I read of his beauty, but it meant nothing to me: it was as if I were blind or in the dark. That is why I became so fond of portraits of our Lord. I loved to gaze on his beauty, as an artist had envisaged it, and let my whole heart and body be enraptured by him.

Falling Asleep

For many years, almost every night as I lay in bed, I would think about the scene of our Lord in the Garden. I could see that painful sweat falling from him. I could feel his anguish. And I prayed that even in my dreams I would be awake to his sacrificial love.

Agony and Joy

As my capacity for prayer developed, I found that in prayer my ordinary mental faculties fell asleep, and my senses grew dim. Then a new feeling, a new sensation, began to rise up through my body to my neck. I was powerless to control this experience: I could not hasten it nor prevent it. I was like a man on the point of dying the death he desires: in his final agony there is overwhelming joy. I was dying to the world, and discovering spiritual delights which I could not have imagined. I did not know what to do, whether to laugh or cry, whether to speak or be silent. It was a glorious confusion, a heavenly madness.

Then I found myself talking and singing to God. I am no poet, but verses seemed to pour from my mouth, filled with the most intense emotion. I expressed to God the acute pain and the most wonderful pleasure. I would gladly have cut myself to pieces, to show the joy I felt in my agony. The greatest torments became my highest joys. I wanted neither to eat nor sleep.

The Nuptial Ecstasy

I began to experience true ecstasy, which I believe to be the highest form of prayer. I was devoting myself especially to the service of others and was constantly thanking God for the many blessings of my life, when suddenly he seemed to seize my soul and lift it upwards through the clouds. Onwards and upwards my soul seemed to travel, racing towards the sun. Then I knew I was entering his kingdom. I cannot describe it because I did not see it with my visual sense; I simply knew it.

I was overwhelmed with joy and sweetness. My body was still present, but was cold and lifeless, no longer animated by the soul. Yet the soul itself was totally and completely alive. There was no way I could resist what was happening. I had no choice but to submit myself to God. My soul was truly Christ's bride, and this was the ecstasy of the nuptial bed.

Christ's Body

One day when I was at prayer, the Lord came to me and showed me his hands. Their beauty was beyond description. I felt very frightened because, although I knew that the Lord was granting me a great favour, the experience was so new. Then a few days later the Lord came to me again and showed me his face. I was utterly entranced. I could not understand why the Lord was revealing himself to me in his body, when I was already so utterly in love with him spiritually. A little later he came to me again, this time showing me his whole self – his hair, face, body, arms and legs. His beauty was far, far beyond the finest portrait that any artist has painted.

I wanted to clasp him to my bosom, to embrace him and kiss him with my lips. But I was in such rapture that I could not move. I asked him why he was granting me this wonderful favour. And as I asked the question, I knew the answer. He was pandering to the weakness of my nature.

For two and a half years he came to me frequently in this physical form. I came to know well the colour of his hair and eyes, the shape of his mouth, and the sound of his voice. Then he stopped coming to me, and no amount of prayer could bring back his physical presence.

The Sharp Burning Spear

I rarely have visits from angels in physical form; but one day the Lord sent an angel to me, to commit the most terrifying, and yet most wonderful, act of violence.

The angel was strange, yet very beautiful. His face was aflame, so I took him to be one of the highest rank of angels whose faces are constantly on fire. In his hands I saw a great golden spear with an iron tip which was red hot. Then he plunged the spear into my heart, thrusting inwards several times so that it penetrated to my entrails. When he pulled it out I felt that he took my entrails with it.

The pain was so severe that I cried out in agony. Yet at the same time I was utterly consumed with the love of God. Indeed the pain and the love were one and the same, giving my whole body a sensation of sharp sweetness. Though I continued to cry out, I wanted the sensation never to cease.

The sensation of sharp sweetness lasted for several days, and I went into a stupor. I had no wish to open my eyes or to speak, but simply to embrace the blissful suffering which the angel had bestowed on me.

I Die Because I Do Not Die

The Lord has claimed me for his own. My heart has been captured by him. So I am dead to the world, estranged from earthly things. I die because I do not die.

He has locked me in a prison from which there is no escape. I am alone, without comfort and solace. My only hope is that he will come to me here. I die because I do not die.

This prison is cold and dark. The hours of the day and night hang heavy. I am held by cruel chains which cut into my arms and legs. I die because I do not die.

Day and night I wait for him. I long for him to come to my dungeon. He alone can bring warmth, light, happiness. May he come quickly to me, or else I shall despair. I die because I do not die.

What Will You Do with Me?

I am yours, because you made me. I am yours, because you saved me. I am yours, because you alone truly love me. What will you do with me?

Sweetest love, I come to you. I want your will to rule my will, your desires to become my desires, your plan to become my plan. What will you do with me?

Take, dear Lord, my loving heart. I submit myself to you. My heart and my body yield to your love. You are my husband and I am your wife. What will you do with me?

Let me live or let me die. Give me sickness or give me health. Give me poverty or give me riches. Make me strong or make me weak. What will you do with me?

Give me fame or give me shame. Punish me or make me happy. Comfort me or sadden me. Send me misery or send me joy. I have given my whole self to you. What will you do with me?

The Divine Huntsman

The divine huntsman shot me through the heart with his arrow of love, and left me lying, faint and weak.

My heart now belonged to him. He came to me, lifted me up, and embraced me.

He plucked the arrow from my heart, telling me the wound would never heal.

So for all eternity I shall suffer the agony of divine love.

The Divine Craftsman

I was created by Love to be loving. I was created by Beauty to be beautiful. I was created by Faith to be faithful. The divine craftsman fashioned me in his image.

If I look into my heart I can see his image of Love, Beauty and Faith. I can see within myself what he wants me to be.

Yet I fail to reflect his image. I have sullied his creation. I am hateful, ugly, faithless.

Divine craftsman, return to me, and re-create me. Let me love you as you should be loved. Let me be beautiful, that you may embrace me as your own. Let me always be your faithful spouse.

Happy, Joyful Bride

What a happy, joyful bride I am! I have won for myself a royal husband, a King above all kings, an Emperor whose empire is the universe.

I have no dowry for him except my loyal heart. I have no gifts for him except my loving soul. In taking me as his bride, he gains nothing.

Yet he shall make me what he wants me to be. He shall turn me into a gift worthy of his love. And my heart shall sing for him the sweetest songs of praise.

The Growth of Love

When I was a tender maiden, you chose me as your bride. I was full of loving ardour, and you captured my heart. You became my husband and my lover.

But the joys of young love do not last. I began to be reviled and insulted because of my passion for you. People mocked me for marrying you.

Then my own heart seemed to grow cold. I still loved you, but I no longer wanted you near me. I still spoke to you, but my words had no meaning.

Yet you remained faithful and never let me go. You did not revive the ardour of young love, but instead filled my heart with a gentle warmth that I knew would last for ever.

Now I always want you near me, because in you I find peace. Now I speak to you constantly, telling you of my every thought, and you listen patiently.

Gentle lover, sweet husband, even in my youthful passion I could never have imagined such joy as this.

Sing to Me

Good Jesus, sing to me the sweet melody and heavenly song of the angels, that I may chant the same words and music to you.

Fondle me with your divine hands, cover me with divine kisses, that I may give to you the fullness of my love.

Show me the beauty of your sweetness and charm, that

reflecting your image I may be sweet and beautiful in your sight.

Clasp me to your bosom, hold me tightly to your body, that I may always be faithful and loyal in my love for you.

JOHN OF THE CROSS

As a young monk he met Teresa of Avila and was enthralled by the erotic mysticism which she taught. He began to see his own relationship with God as akin to that between two lovers. And the sexual imagery in his poetry is even more explicit than that in Teresa's works. Like Teresa of Avila his inner ecstasy gave him boundless energy, and in his relatively short life – he died in 1591 in his fiftieth year – he founded fifteen new monasteries.

Pain and Joy

On a dark night, with the flame of desire burning within me,
I went secretly to my beloved's house.

I ran through the darkness, opened my lover's door, and
    climbed the stairs,
Up to his room, my heart ablaze with desire.

O happy blessed night, O moment of serene delight:
It was an eternal light which guided me to my eternal
    beloved's arms.

I was transformed by love, I was driven mad by love;
Lover and beloved were made one in the joy of that sacred
  night.

He laid his head upon my breast, as if my breast was a bed
  of flowers;
And I caressed his sacred head, stroking his soft, shiny
  hair.

Then I saw wounds on his hands and feet, terrible gaping
  holes in his flesh;
I knew that these were wounds of love, suffered for my
  sake.

As I gazed upon his wounds, I shared his agony,
  screaming with pain.
Yet in that pain my heart and my body filled with ecstatic
  joy.

All worldly thought were driven from my mind, as I lay
  with my lover.
Only the joy of his loving sacrifice remained.

Together and Apart

LOVER:

Where has my lover vanished, leaving my heart full of
  sorrow?
Like a deer he has run away from me, leaving me weeping
  with grief.

Shepherds, when you walk with your sheep across the
hills, please look for him.
And if you see my lover, tell him that I am dying of
sorrow.

I myself will look for him on the hills and in the valleys.
I won't stop to pick flowers, and I will not fear any wild
animals.

O trees, O flowers, O hedges, have you seen my lover
come this way?
O fields, O ditches, has my lover, handsome and strong,
crossed you?

I wish my grief would end; I wish this sorrow would turn
again to joy.
You, dear lover, and you alone, can bring me happiness,
satisfying my every desire.

The flowers and the animals tell me of your beauty and
your grace;
But to be reminded of you only increases the pain of
separation.

Why have you pierced my heart with such grief, why have
you caused me such pain?
Have pity on me, end my torment, pierce me with love.

BELOVED:

I am returning to you, my love. Lift your eyes and look up
to the hills.
Then you will see me, running towards you.

211

LOVER:

My love is like the first light of dawn and the last light of
dusk.
He is like the first and the last note of the most exquisite
song.

Make ready our nuptial bed. Spread a sheet of royal purple
upon it.
And surround our bed with the most fragrant flowers.

When my lover first gave himself to me, teaching me the
secret science of love,
I knew that I would always belong to him, and him alone.

He lavished his love on me, giving all and keeping nothing
back.
And love became my only labour and my only pleasure.

I want no other work, no other joy, than to give myself to
him.
Without him I have nothing and am nothing; with him I
have all I desire.

I know that I am ugly and ungainly, unworthy of such a
man.
Yet his beauty makes me beautiful, his grace makes me
graceful.

BELOVED

Come into my garden, and rest in the shade of the trees.
Let me embrace you, as you sit beneath the spring blossoms.

I will put my hand in yours, promising always to be with you.
Even when I am far away, I shall still be close to you.

I will play my lyre and sing songs of love for you.
The birds will join my song, and even the wild beasts will roar with delight.

Just as you have been grieving now, you will grieve again in the future.
Just as I seemed far away from you now, I will seem to flee in the future.

But I seem to leave you in order that our love is stronger when I return.
Be faithful to me in these times of sorrow, and then our love will be infinitely joyful.

Yet at this moment, lie back and enjoy our love.
Let all sorrow flee from your mind, and let your body be filled with pleasure.

Living Fire

O living fire of love, you burn in the very centre of my soul.
The pains of your flames are my joy; the wounds which you inflict are my delight.

You consume all that is dead within me, you destroy all that is evil.
Every part of my soul which you touch is brought to life.

In your warmth I can sense pleasures beyond all imagination.
I can feel within your blaze joy beyond my dreams.

How tender is the love awakening within me; how sweet are its delights.
You are my secret lover, invisible to others, yet all in all to me.

ISLAM

INTRODUCTION: ISLAM

According to the Koran, the Muslim holy book, men who reach Paradise will recline on soft couches set with jewels, drinking the finest wines and be surrounded by beautiful women. Meanwhile on earth wine is forbidden, but the devout Muslim is encouraged to have a full-blooded attitude to sexuality.

Muhammed himself, the founder of Islam, was a rather austere young man; but in his later years, when he was widely hailed both as a prophet and a political leader, his sexual potency was remarkable. He did not marry until the age of 25, and then to a widow fifteen years older. They lived faithfully together for twenty-four years until her death. When he began to go out at night to a mountain cave to receive the divine revelations which form the Koran, she was the first to believe in his prophetic gift; and on his return in the morning, when he was tense and exhausted, she comforted him with sexual intercourse. By the time of her death Muhammed was the virtual ruler of Arabia, at the head of a victorious army. His followers now expected him, like any other Arab leader, to enjoy his success by taking numerous wives and concubines.

Muhammed happily obliged, and in the final twelve years of his life fathered countless children by many different women.

The Koran contains numerous verses about the sexual relations between men and women. It takes for granted that sexual activity is an important part of human life, and it seeks only to regulate for the best interests of society as a whole. In particular, since many young men are killed in battle, it urges the surviving men to take a number of wives, ensuring that all women of marriageable age are cared for. The only controls on such polygamy are the man's wealth and the danger of quarrelling amongst rival wives. Prior to sexual intercourse the man should utter a prayer; then he should concentrate on giving himself and the woman the maximum pleasure.

Islam accords great respect to the Sunna, the tradition which developed after Muhammed's death. On sexual matters, as on other issues, the Sunna is more specific than the Koran. Celibacy is actually forbidden, and the Sunna declares that 'the whole world is to be enjoyed, and the best thing in the world is a good woman'. Women for their part are required to submit to their husbands' desires; and a husband may even divorce a wife who refuses intercourse at least once a week. Men are also allowed intercourse with slave girls captured in war, but should avoid letting the slave girl conceive by withdrawing the penis before ejaculation. The wise man should increase his pleasure by adopting a wide variety of positions for intercourse; but on no account should he penetrate the woman's anus, as this will cause a child to be born with a squint.

Islam rapidly spread across the entire Middle East, and soon had its own literature. Not surprisingly, many of the stories that were written involve sex, treating the subject with both wit and insight, and a large number were eventually collected in the famous *Thousand and One Nights*. Manuals were also published with such titles as *The Mysteries of Married Love* and *The Compendium of Pleasure*. Sadly most of these are lost, but the most famous manual, *The Perfumed Garden*, is equal to its Hindu counterparts.

Islam in its original form is a robust, practical faith. But once it began to absorb other cultural influences, especially in Persia, it acquired its own mystical tradition. Known as Sufis, the great Islamic mystics composed some of the finest religious poetry in the world. And much of it is intensely erotic, with God regarded as 'the Beloved' and the mystic seeing himself as 'the Lover'.

SANA'I

God – or Allah – was to this restless Persian mystic the 'Beloved', to whom he wrote passionate love poems. Born in the capital city in 1070, he began his career as a poet in the sultan's court where he was greatly admired. But on a journey with the sultan he made contact with Sufi mystical groups, whose spiritual devotion impressed him. He decided to abandon the comforts of the palace and spent thirty years wandering across Persia, in search of wisdom. Eventually he returned home, where he met and married an old woman, who at last brought him contentment.

Love's Prisoner

Your love gives life to my soul.
Your majesty inflicts death on my pride.
Wherever you are, most beautiful Being,
I am joyful and free of care.

I love your divine loveliness.
Your smile is more intoxicating than wine.

Under your gaze my limbs go weak,
And I fall into delicious slumber.

If only I could kiss your hand,
My bliss would reach up to the heavens.
I would be richer than the richest king,
Happier than the happiest queen.

Hourly I yearn to kiss your lips,
My heart is a prisoner to love.
I cannot think about worldly affairs,
My mind can think only of you.

My nose seems to smell your fragrance,
As if you were walking close by.
Come to me, show yourself to me,
And I shall be happy for ever.

Vain Hope

Who am I, that for even one instant
You should give a thought to me?
What right have I even to desire
The love of one so exalted as you?

If only my spirit were worthy
Of one moment of your attention,
Then I would have received
Happiness to last a lifetime.

Every breath which my body breathes
Is a sigh of desire.

Every beat which my heart beats
Is a reminder of you.

But I know that my life is wasted,
I know what I hope is vain.
I could search the entire world,
And still I would not find you.

I look for your face and see nothing.
I look for your shadow and see nothing.
I look for your footsteps and see nothing
Not even a hint of you can I see.

I am too lowly to eat at your table;
Too ugly to be met by your eyes;
Too sinful to be in your presence.
My hope for your love is in vain.

Beholding My Beloved

When I behold my Beloved
My life becomes a festival.
When I welcome my Beloved
My house becomes a palace.

On the breeze my Beloved's fragrance
Is carried into my garden.
Every flower, every herb and tree
Smells of my Beloved.

When I walk into my fields
And wander amidst the corn,

222

I can hear my Beloved's whisper
As the stalks rustle in the wind.

When I walk amongst my trees
And watch the birds flying above,
I can hear my Beloved's voice
As the nightingale sings her anthem.

When I lie on my soft lawn
And feel the sun shine on me,
I can feel my Beloved's breath
In the warm air on my face.

When I rest on my bed at night
And draw the sheets up over me,
I can feel my Beloved's caress
In the soft touch of the silk.

The Ocean of Love

What is love? A mighty ocean
Whose waters heave and roll.
Waves rise up like mountains
Then collapse into deep valleys.

In the swell of Divine Love
I am lifted to the heights of joy.
Then suddenly I am cast down
Into the depths of misery.

Huge fish lurk in the ocean
With shiny scales of blue and silver.

They have teeth like sharp swords,
And jaws as strong as death.

In the teeth of Divine Love
I have been clasped.
Love rose up and gripped me,
And now I cannot swim free.

Pity the ships on the ocean
Bobbing in the blue-white waves.
Their sailors pray for safety
Lest the sea swallow them up.

Love tosses me upwards and down,
I am sick with love's restless motion.
But I no longer pray for safety.
May I drown in the ocean of Love.

The Road to Love

I tried to draw a map
Of the road to the home of Love.
I trusted the power of intellect
To lead me to the home of Love.

I thought my map was right
And boldly I started the journey.
With a confident smile on my face
I stepped along the path.

But Love came and took my hand.
Her grip was warm and soft.

She told me she would show the way
To her home where happiness reigns.

She led me off the road
Through dark and dank forests,
Over mountains white with snow,
By valleys green and lush.

She took the map from my hand
And threw it to the winds.
I felt angry, anxious and lost.
She was forcing me to trust her.

But at last we reached her home.
She laid me on her bed.
All thoughts vanished from my head.
Now I was ready for love.

Old, Grey Love

Once I was liked by all,
The most popular man in the town.
When I sat in the market-square
Crowds gathered round me.

People listened to my every word,
They believed I spoke with wisdom.
They laughed at my witty remarks,
They were sad when I went home.

But I knew my wisdom was false.
I knew my wit was empty.

I was liked, but had no love.
My heart was cold and dark.

So one day I left my town,
Said farewell to all my friends.
They cried to see me go,
But in truth I despised their folly.

For thirty years I searched.
I walked across the world,
Seeking the woman who could open
The divine secrets of love.

At last I returned to my town,
Weary, old and grey.
I married an old, grey woman,
The only one who would have me.

I wanted her to cook and clean,
But with her I found true love.
In our gentle, quiet embraces
God revealed his deepest mystery.

ATTAR

His personal name was Abu-Talib, but he adopted the name Attar, meaning 'pharmacist', partly because he earned his living dispensing medicines, and partly because he regarded his poetry as medicine for the soul. In the latter years of the twelfth century he travelled widely from Egypt to India, seeking the wisdom of holy men, but for the last forty years of his life he settled back in his native town in northeastern Persia. His poems are marked by strong naturalistic images, including many sexual metaphors.

A Storm, A Candle, A Road

Imagine a storm at sea.
The waves are rising as high as mountains.
Each has a crest of pure, white foam.
Then imagine the sea catches fire.
The waves are red with heat.
The crest of foam is flames leaping upwards.
That is how I feel for the Beloved.
My heart rises high, and is ablaze with desire.
My soul and body leap up to heaven.

Imagine a candle burning at night.
The night is dark, cold and still.
The flame of the wick is the only light on earth.
Then imagine a high wind starts to blow.
The candle's flame flickers in the gale.
But, though sometimes it seems to die, it always re-ignites.
That is how I feel for the Beloved.
Outwardly my life is joyless, but inwardly I burn.
No suffering, no calamity can extinguish my love.

Imagine a long, winding road.
It is rough, hard and stony.
It passes through deserts and forests, over mountains and
  valleys.
Then imagine a few people walking along it.
They rarely speak, and look weak and weary.
But by day and night they continue their journey.
That is how I feel for the Beloved.
Slowly, yet surely, I follow the Beloved's Way.
There are others with me, and soon all joy will be
  ours.

A Single Raindrop

A single raindrop fell from the sky.
It came down in the middle of the sea.
It merged into the waters so no-one could see it.
Fish swam past it, boats sailed past it.
Yet the raindrop remembered where it had been,
And always hoped it would one day return to the sky.

My soul came down from heaven.
I am now forced to live in the world.
My life is the same as any other person's
People walk past me, jostle me in the marketplace.
Yet I remember the joys of heaven,
And one day I shall return.

In the world there is one great joy.
The warm, soft love of a woman.
Men will cheat and kill in pursuit of that joy.
But I remember an even greater joy,
The inextinguishable love of the Beloved.
And that joy is given freely to those who can receive.

I am no better than any other person.
No-one respects me as wise or profound.
I am a raindrop like any other.
But I treasure my heavenly memories, while others forget.
Others seek pleasure in an earthly body,
I wait for joy with a Heavenly Being.

The Nectar of Truth

The bees buzz from flower to flower.
Through the summer they are buzzing,
They take the honey and carry it to their nest.
They store for themselves the sweetest food that Nature
   knows.
When their nest is overflowing, in the autumn,
They drink their fill of honey, and more.
They fly from their nest drunk with sweetness.
Their buzz is now deep, delirious with joy.

Throughout my life I have sought the wisdom of the
   wise.
I have gone from person to person seeking truth.
I have stored their insights and pondered them deeply,
Hoping that I would find the secret of divine bliss.
But though my mind was full of wise words,
My heart was still empty, cold and joyless.
So I stopped travelling to wise men,
And I ceased my search for truth.

Then a strange and wonderful thing began to happen.
I could feel a buzz within my heart.
The divine spirit was gathering my passions and emotions,
And bringing them together in a single desire.
Soon my heart was overflowing with joyful love,
And into my body the nectar surged.
I was drunk with desire for the Beloved.
I had found within me the universal truth.

The Door and the Veil

I stood behind a heavy door.
It was closed and locked.
Once I had possessed the key,
But long ago I had lost it.

Beyond that door I remembered a veil
Of crimson, shiny silk.
Behind that veil lies the Beloved,
Beautiful, enticing, ready to love.

I could choose to wait here,
Sad, miserable, with desire unfulfilled.
Or I could try to make a key,
And open the door, and lift the veil.

Dimly I could recall the key's shape.
So I began to make a new key.
My heart beating with excitement,
I pushed the key in the lock.

The door slowly swung open,
Creaking, groaning, scraping.
I crept into the chamber,
And lifted the silk, crimson veil.

I treasure that key as my life.
I frequently return to the Beloved.
The joys I receive in that chamber
Make the burdens of the world seem light.

RUMI

Commonly regarded as the greatest Muslim poet, he took his name from the town in Asia Minor where he grew up. As a young man he studied theology, but under the influence of a wandering teacher who visited his town he gave up theology for a passionate form of mysticism. He founded the Mevlevi order of 'dancing dervishes' who sought God through frenzied, ecstatic dancing. His poetry, which often takes the form of mystical riddles, expresses his devotion to God as his 'Beloved'. He died in Konge in 1273.

Head below Feet

Today I saw the Beloved, the object of every heart's desire.
The sun is put to shame by the Beloved's beauty: the moon
 is shamed by the Beloved's soft glow.
I said: 'Show me the way to Heaven.'
The Beloved replied: 'Bring your head below your feet, so
 the foot of love will be your highest place.'
I understood the Beloved to mean that I must no longer be
 ruled by thought, but only by love.

The Time for Union

Lovers, lovers, the time for union has come.

So let your hearts be joyful, let your bodies leap with
   gladness.

The demon of sadness has been banished, and even the
   heavens are drunk with passion.

Let every minstrel play the music of divine pleasure.

Let even the reeds blowing in the wind sound a happy
   note.

Lovers, lovers, jump on your steeds of desire, and ride
   towards the one who satisfies.

To a Dry Lip

To a dry lip my Beloved is like a fountain in the desert.

To a tired body my Beloved is like the gentle breeze at
   dusk.

To a sad heart my Beloved is like the sweet song of the
   nightingale.

To a hungry belly my Beloved is like the finest bread.

To a man without love my Beloved is love itself.

Fish in the Sea

Have you ever seen a fish that was satiated with the sea?

I am never satiated with my Beloved's love.

Have you ever seen an image fleeing from the engraver?

I never flee from my Beloved's beauty.

My Beloved is the sea, and I am a fish within it.

My Beloved is the engraver, and I am his image.

The Beloved's Lance

My Beloved came to me, lance in hand, and said: 'What
 service can I render?'
I was frightened and I started to flee.
But passion rose within me and I said: 'Pierce me with
 your lance that I may suffer the agony of love.'
My Beloved pierced me, and I never recovered.

My Master and Mistress

Reason is my master; my mind is constantly seeking
 explanations for things.
Talk is my mistress; my voice is constantly asking
 questions and giving answers.
Reason and words are barriers, holding back the passion
 within the heart.
Wrap my mind and my voice in a shroud, and bury them
 in a cemetery.
Then let passion be my master and my mistress.

Soul and Heart

My soul is a stranger to my heart.
My heart is in love, it beats with desire at the thought of
 my Beloved.
But my soul is dull and lifeless. It wants nothing because it
 feels nothing.
My heart wants to pass every day sitting with my Beloved
 by a beautiful stream, singing sweet songs of love.

My soul can do no more than utter stale prayers by rote,
   without any sense of their meaning.
My heart enjoys my Beloved; but my soul refuses to make
   sacrifices for my Beloved.

A Sharp Dagger

If you are in love with the Beloved, do not try to find
   reasons for your love.
Take a sharp dagger, and cut the throat of reason; then
   you will go mad with love.
If you are in love with the Beloved, do not try to describe
   the Beloved's beauty.
Take a sharp dagger, and cut the throat of wordiness; let
   beauty be its own description.
If you are in love with the Beloved, do not be shy or
   bashful.
Take a sharp dagger, and cut the throat of caution; then
   throw yourself into the Beloved's arms.

Love and Peace

I remember when I would lie down at night, and drift into
   restful, dreamless sleep.
Now there is no peace even in sleep, for my Beloved fills
   the night with dreams.
There is joy and pleasure in these dreams, but no rest or
   peace.
I cannot escape my Beloved, but I yearn for rest.
Is it possible to be both in love, and at peace?

The Water-Wheel

The river runs beside the mill, but the water-wheel refuses
    to turn.
So the paddles beneath the water grow green and rot,
    while those above grow grey and dry.
Once my heart spun with love, and every part of me was
    healthy and vigorous.
Now my heart refuses to turn at the sight of my Beloved,
    even when he passes close by.
For much of the time I feel grey and dry, my heart
    shrivelling in the hot sun.
But in the depths of my being I am decaying, for I am
    spiritually sick.

Others Tell Me So

My Beloved is very beautiful: others tell me so.
There is no greater joy than being seduced by the Beloved:
    others tell me so.
The Beloved is soft and gentle, yet firm and strong; others
    tell me so.
If I sit down and think hard, I can remember from my own
    experience all these things.
But now these memories are dust: I see nothing, I want
    nothing, I feel nothing.

Chains Snapping

Today I am going mad: I can feel chains snapping in my
head.

All night I have wandered through the city, unable to
sleep.

The Beloved has been inside my head, dancing and
clapping.

Now the Beloved is seizing the chains which hold my
thoughts together, and breaking them.

Will I die, or will I come back to life?

Love is like a Tree

Love is like a tree.

Its roots reach out together in one direction before time;
and in the other direction beyond time.

In its trunk are all feelings and passions, all desires and
longings.

In winter feelings and passions, desires and longings are
trapped within the trunk, and the tree seems lifeless.

Then in the spring feelings and passions, desires and
longings break out in glorious blossom.

They bring beauty which, even though seen before, never
ceases to astonish those who behold it.

And in time those blossoms turn into the most delicious
fruit.

Its sweetness, though tasted before, never ceases to
entrance those who enjoy it.

The winter returns, to be followed again by spring and
summer.

The Bird of My Heart

The bird of my heart has again begun to flutter; I can feel
the beat of its wings.

The parrot of my soul has again begun to chew sugar; I can
taste its sweetness.

The camel of my mind has again begun to pull at its chains;
I know that reason is escaping.

At last I can once more feel passion for the Beloved.

At last I can once more enjoy the pleasures the Beloved
bestows.

At last I know once more the real happiness that comes
from loving the Beloved.

Love is like a Reed Pipe

Love is like a reed pipe, blown by the Beloved.

The note of one reed goes straight into the heart, and
inspires passion.

The note of another reed goes straight into the body, and
inspires desire.

The note of another reed goes straight into the soul, and
inspires devotion.

The note of another reed goes straight into the mind, and
inspires poetry.

Let me feel my Beloved's breath come into me.

My Lance in My Hand

I am holding my lance in my hand: it is strong, firm and
   long.
I am in a fury of love, a rage of passion.
I want to pierce my Beloved, to penetrate to the very heart
   of my Beloved.
Will my Beloved resist me, fight me, throw me back?
Or will my Beloved receive my passion and accept the
   wounds my love inflicts?
My Beloved will only be pierced by me if I am pierced by
   the Beloved.

The Way to the Beloved

Do not ask me the way to my Beloved.
I want all people to find the way, but it cannot be
   described.
The way to the Beloved, the path to the house of the
   Beloved, is the house itself.
So it is impossible to tell you the way without telling you
   about the Beloved.
The Beloved has beauty beyond words, and embodies joy
   beyond reason.
Yet at times that beauty seems like ugliness beyond the
   worst nightmare, and the joy turns to misery.
I cannot explain that change, because in truth nothing has
   changed.
There is no other way but that of beauty and ugliness, joy
   and misery.

HAFIZ

His name is a title given to him as a theologian, indicating that he knew by heart the Koran, the Muslim sacred text, and understood its inner meaning. As well as writing theological tracts, he was poet to the royal court in Shiraz, the Persian capital. His poems, known as 'ghazals', were short verses which could be read on two levels. At the superficial level they were celebrations of life's pleasures, especially wine and women; at a deeper level they were mystical attempts to penetrate the divine mystery. He died in 1390 as the Persian empire was collapsing in the face of Mongol invasions.

Drunk with Love

I look for you, but I cannot find you.
I desire you, but fear of you inhibits me.
If I could kiss you, I would be drunk with the wine of love.
If I could embrace you, my soul would melt into yours.

You Are All

You can only be embraced by those who do not want to
   possess you.
You can only be loved by those who want to love all
   humanity.
You cannot be confined in any house, any palace, any
   garden.
You are everywhere, always, for all people.

I Have No Gold

I have no gold, no silver, and no rubies to give you.
But when I speak to you, you tell me that my words are as
   bright as gold.
When I sing to you, you tell me my voice is as clear as
   silver.
When I kiss you, you tell me my lips are as beautiful as
   rubies.

The Salty Desert

In the salty deserts of the world, a man only knows
   sorrow.
Human love is nothing but a snare to capture and kill the
   heart.
In their hearts most men curse the day when they were
   born.
Even when their faces are smiling and laughing, their
   souls are weeping.

SACRED SEX

Firm, Sharp, Soft, Round

Who was it, Beloved, who designed your features, so firm
and so sharp?
Who was it, Beloved, who designed your shape, so soft
and so round?
When you speak to me your words are firm and sharp,
guiding my every action.
When you speak to me your tone is soft and round,
soothing away my fears.

Like a Beggar

Like a beggar, I cling tightly to your robes.
I plead with you to look upon me with kindness.
But unlike a beggar I do not want food or drink.
I am hungry and thirsty for your love.

I Am Your Slave

I am resigned to be a slave of you who loves me.
I have no choice but to wear your rope around my neck,
I will drink and eat only what you give me.
My happiness shall consist of crumbs of love from your
table.

A Lute and a Pipe

As if I was playing a lute, I caress your hair.
Each curl is like a string which I pluck.
Beloved, breathe on me as if you were playing a pipe.
Blow your sweet breath into my soul.

Three Fires

I have learnt that there are three fires, which look the
  same, but feel quite different.
There are the fires of hell, which burn when I am apart
  from you.
There is the fire of passion, which burns when I am close
  to you.
And there is the purifying fire, which makes me ready to
  love you.

A Nightingale and a Rose

My heart is like a nightingale singing the sweetest songs to
  you.
My mind is like a rose reflecting your divine beauty.
There are many who want to cut the bird's throat and
  pluck the rose.
Those who love you have many enemies.

In Your Street

In your street no-one is poor and homeless.
In your street no-one is lonely and friendless.
Even those who have nothing find a home in your heart.
Even those who are surrounded by enemies find a friend
  and protector in you.

Heat and Coolness

When I am hot with love, a breeze blows over me to cool
  my body.
When I am cold with sadness, the warm sun shines to
  warm my body.
You are my breeze and you are my sun.
You bring coolness and heat at the right times.

In a Pool of Tears

In a pool of tears I will lie tonight.
Far away from your bed of love I will lie tonight.
I will lie, but my eyes will be open, unable to sleep.
Every night without you is a night without rest.

A Worthless Fortune

To gain a world's fortune through tyranny is worthless.
Even to gain a fortune through fair and honest means is
  worthless.
No amount of gold, silver and jewels can bring a moment's
  true joy.
Only your love, my Beloved, has any value.

Is This Heaven?

We sit together by a clear, crystal stream.
Beside us is a jug of wine.
Our hands clasp, our lips touch.
Is this heaven?
Is this what all the sages, in every place at every time, have
  promised?

Sweet Talk, Handsome Faces

Those who talk sweetly often make promises they do not
  keep.
Those with handsome faces and lithe figures are often
  impotent in both body and soul.
I am a poor speaker, but the words of love which I offer to
  you are true.
I am ugly and weak, but all that I am belongs to you.

Divine Beauty

The curl in your hair, what has caused it?
The sparkle in your eye, what has caused it?
The shine in your cheek, what has caused it?
It is impossible to explain beauty which is truly divine.

Being Passive

I grasped at your robe, hoping to obtain what the robe
    contains.
I tried to pull off your belt, hoping to have my way with
    you.
But a man can only receive from you what you want to
    give.
To receive your love a man must be passive.

Praise and Glory

It is truly a great mistake to glorify oneself.
It is the height of folly to heap praise upon one's own gifts.
The only glory worth receiving is that which is reflected
    from you.
The only gifts worth possessing are those which satisfy
    your desire for love.

The Bowl of Love

If you wished, you could gather the whole world into a
  bowl.
Then you could pound it, pummel it, crush it until it was
  reduced to dust.
My Beloved, gather me into the bowl of your love.
Then pound me, pummel me, crush me, until I am wholly
  yours.

The Juice of Love

I am wholly enchanted, I am weak from so much love.
I lie here on your bed, like fruit that has dried in the sun.
There is no more juice within me, no more love to offer.
Yet if you want more, you can fill me with juice.

A Dark Mole

I thought I saw a dark mole on you.
I thought that there was a blemish on your beauty.
But as my eyes moved up and down, and side to side, the
  mole moved too.
Then I realized the blemish was in my eye, not on you.

Past, Present, Future

The only aim of my love is to satisfy you.
The only source of my joy is to make you joyful.
When I think of yesterday, today and tomorrow, I realize
  you are my past, present and future.
Let me grow in passion as the years pass.

Real Dreams

Every morning I tell you all the secrets of my heart.
I tell you how during the night I have dreamt of you and
  desired you.
Yet you know these secrets even before I tell you.
My dreams were real, my desires were satisfied.

THE PERFUMED GARDEN

The author, Nefzawi, of this famous Muslim sex manual, written in the sixteenth century, was undoubtedly familiar with the sex manuals of India. Yet the work has a distinctive Islamic spirit. Sex is seen as a gift from God, which should be enjoyed according to his plan. Thus the book assumes a strict morality in which intercourse takes place within marriage, and should be the expression of love and – more importantly – mutual respect. Nefzawi saw sex as an art to be learnt; and if practised with skill it could reflect God's beauty as vividly as the murals which decorated the great mosques. The most striking section of the book is that which deals with sex for 'men and women with extreme differences': Nefzawi is concerned that everyone, including the disabled, should enjoy the divine gift.

God's Sexual Plan

May God be praised for so ordering human nature that man's greatest pleasure lies in satisfying women's desires, and that women's greatest pleasure lies in satisfying man's desires. God has not given women's sexual organs any joy until they have been united with man's; and man's sexual organs find their joy in unity with women's.

When men and women come together for this God-given pleasure, they engage in an amorous battle, pulling and pushing each other this way and that. God has given men and women the pleasure of kissing as they wrestle, which provokes the man's penis to grow and makes the woman's vulva moist. God has also given woman two soft breasts to be admired, fondled and kissed by the man, which further stimulates the penis and the vulva.

God has made the vulva itself like the lower part of a human face. It has two lips, a mouth and a tongue. Just as men and women can speak words of love with their actual tongues, so the tongue of the vulva expresses that love in becoming firm and erect, beckoning the man to enter.

Now the amorous combat nears its climax. The man's penis is like a lance, and when it pierces the vulva man and woman fight like two soldiers on the battlefield. God watches with joy because, whereas soldiers fight with grim faces and hurt each other, men and women smile and laugh as they fight, giving pleasure to one another as the man thrusts his weapon into the woman.

Finally, if men and women do battle with skill and artistry, both will be victorious at one and the same time. And after the happy victory even the strongest men and most vigorous women lie back, utterly weakened and exhausted. May God be praised for creating such a delightful combat!

What a Woman Despises and Admires

A woman does not look for physical prowess in a man. To many women a man heavy with muscles is ugly and unattractive. Besides, when he lies on her she will feel his weight on her breasts and belly, and hardly be able to breathe.

A woman despises a man who lies on her and penetrates without first playing with her. A woman is slow to reach her peak of desire, and only when she is approaching that peak should she be penetrated. So the man who penetrates her quickly may even cause her pain. And he will be ready to reach his climax when in her the fire of desire is just beginning to burn. He will climb off her exhausted and satisfied, while she is just ready to begin. She will come to hate a man that constantly leaves her unsatisfied.

A woman despises the man who, once he has penetrated her, only thrusts hard and fast. Even if he has played with her first, bringing her to a peak of desire, he will leave her unsatisfied. This is because he will reach his climax quickly, while the fire within her is still raging.

A woman loves and respects a man with grace and courtesy, who by his manner shows her that he regards her needs and desires as important as his own. Such a man need not be handsome or strong, because his attitude to her will make him beautiful and attractive in her eyes.

The grace and courtesy in his manner must express itself in skill and artistry in coitus. A woman loves a man who can play with her like a musician plays an instrument,

251

plucking the strings of her desire from the lowest to the highest. He kisses her first on the mouth, while his hands caress her face and hair. Then his mouth and hands move to other parts of the body, playing on each part a higher note of desire. Only when she is ready does he reach those parts where the note of desire plays highest, the breasts and the vulva. A woman loves and respects a man who understands how to play with her by observing the movements and responses of her body, without his needing even to speak.

A woman loves and respects a man even more highly if, once he has penetrated her, the music of love has variety of pace and pitch. A man does not know such music by instinct, but, like a true musician, must be willing patiently to learn from the artistry of those who have gone before.

Thus above all a woman loves and respects a man who regards sensual love as part of his religion, through which he learns to praise and glorify God. We do not expect to learn the mysteries of faith on our own, but we read books which contain the ancient and eternal wisdom, and we listen to sages who can expound and interpret that wisdom. The art and skill of sensual love is part of that wisdom, to be acquired in the same way as every other part. If a man wishes to be loved and respected by a woman he must be humble in seeking that wisdom.

What a Man Despises and Desires

A man despises a woman who is constantly meddling with matters which are of no concern to her, running to her neighbours to hear and speak idle gossip, plaguing her husband with complaints, and accepting gifts from anyone and everyone. Worst of all he despises a woman who passes on to others the secrets of their marriage bed.

A man despises a woman who is always miserable, with a sombre frown on her face; who is malicious, enjoying lies and foul talk about others; who betrays confidences; who uses coarse language; and who eats her food like a hog. Worst of all he despises a woman who tells malicious stories about him, and tells others of his anxieties and troubles.

A man despises a woman who makes no attempt to please him by what she wears; who appears before him in the morning with unkempt hair and unwashed face; who is untidy, allowing the house to become dirty; and who indulges disgusting personal habits in her husband's presence. Worst of all, he despises a woman who adorns herself for other men and makes the house clean and tidy to receive them, while making no effort for her husband.

A man despises a woman who stimulates his desire with kisses and caresses, but then goes cold, refusing to satisfy his desire; who at times is sexually eager, but at other times makes all sorts of excuses to resist her husband's advances; who grows colder and colder as the years pass until she has no interest in physical pleasure; and who allows her body to become dirty and repulsive, in order to discourage her husband. Worst of all a man despises a woman who makes her religious duties an excuse for her coldness, saying that she can only worship God if she rejects him.

A man loves the woman who enjoys making their home beautiful and pleasing in his eyes; who is so concerned for his needs that she has no interest in other people's affairs; and who is discreet, keeping to herself the joys and the sorrows of the marriage bed.

A man loves the woman who has a warm smile on her face, especially when she sees him; who is tender and gentle, even when her own mood is sad and anxious; who is polite and gracious in her speech, showing appreciation of all his little favours; and who ensures the food he eats is tasty to the eye, the nose and the tongue.

A man loves the woman who dresses each day with the same care as she did on her wedding day; who appears before him in the morning only when her hair is combed, her face washed, and her breath sweet; who treats him with the same seductive charm that she used when she first tried to woo him; who is faithful, looking only to him for her pleasure.

A man loves the woman who can gently stimulate his desire, even when he is tense from hard work, with kisses and caresses; who will satisfy his desire with every kind of sexual play, so that his tension melts into blissful rest; who becomes more creative and imaginative in her lovemaking as the years pass, so the flame of youth is carried into maturity; and who ensures that her body is always clean and fragrant, ready to receive him.

Above all, a man loves the woman whose sexual joy is also religious joy; who knows that in satisfying her husband, she is giving glory to God. God gave us sexual love as a reflection of his love for all mankind. So when a woman gives her love to a man, she is responding to God's love for her.

Preparing for Love

When you approach your wife do not immediately seek to unite your sexual parts. Even if you are ready, she needs time for her vulva to become moist and her clitoris firm. Excite her by kissing her cheeks and lips, and then her stomach and thighs. And as she becomes excited, gently bite her as you kiss. Interlace your legs with hers, and press your breast onto hers. Then touch, kiss and suck her bosoms and her vulva; but if she beckons that she is not yet ready for this, draw back and continue kissing other parts of her body for a few moments longer.

As you excite her, watch and enjoy her responses. She will start to breathe more deeply, and when you hold her close you will feel her heart pounding hard and fast. Her lips will go red, and she will hold her mouth half open. She will move her body this way and that, freely and without inhibition. If you observe your wife carefully, you will soon come to know when it is the right moment for your sexual organs to become fully united.

In teaching the art of love, sages have compared the woman with many things. She is like a fruit which will not yield its sweetness until you rub it between your hands.

She is like the basil plant, which only gives its fragrance when you make it warm by squeezing and rubbing it between your fingers. She is like amber, which, unless it is made hot in the clasp of your hand, keeps hidden within its pores its beautiful aroma. The sweet fragrance of a woman's love can only be enjoyed if you warm her with kisses and caresses.

In truth the act of love is in this respect like the act of prayer. When you kneel before God to offer your devotion, you are not instantly ready to receive his grace. Yet as you concentrate your mind upon him, gradually his warm love infuses you, and you can feel his grace touching every part of your being. Those who are wise and skilled in the art of prayer are frequently excited by God to the degree of enjoying the most ecstatic raptures. When you come to your wife, treat her as God treats you.

The Divers Manners of Love

God wants men and women to enjoy sexual pleasure in the act of sexual union. If one or other person is selfish, trying to gain pleasure without giving it, then in truth neither will receive pleasure. Their marriage will wither, like fruit on a tree deprived of rain, and they will come to find one another repulsive. Yet if both are generous, each eager to give the greatest pleasure to the other, then their mutual joy is enhanced.

The years and decades of a generous marriage will be like the growth of rich fruit on a healthy tree. At first there will be beautiful blossom, which feasts the eye but cannot fully satisfy the body. This blossom proves to be the promise of much better things to come. When the fruit is fully grown, it is not as attractive to the eye as spring blossom, but it is succulent in the mouth and satisfying to the body. So too young love, when men and women court and marry, is wonderful to see because the couple take such delight in each other's youthful charm. Mature love, when men and women have spent years learning to give each other pleasure and joy, may not be so enthralling to watch, but offers true fulfilment to both body and soul.

Generosity in love is first a matter for the soul. Just as God wants the greatest happiness for all his creatures, so men and women must want the greatest happiness for one another. Then it is a matter for the body: to give and receive such happiness requires bodily skill and artistry. Even the most generous men and women can find that love becomes dull and dreary if they act in the same way on each occasion. Just as the tree needs water for the fruit to grow, so love needs variety for the pleasure to grow. God himself has said that the woman is the man's field, where he should play with the greatest skill.

To acquire the skill you must learn the eleven manners of sexual union.

The first manner. The woman lies on her back with her thighs raised. The man, getting between her legs, enters her. Pressing his toes to the ground he can move within her, exploring her as he wants.

The second manner. The woman lies on her back and lifts her legs in the air so her knees come towards her ears.

Her buttocks are now raised and her vulva projects forwards, so the man can easily enter her.

The third manner. The woman stretches herself on the ground, and the man comes between her thighs. He puts one of her legs upon his shoulder and lifts the other under his arm near the armpit, and then gets into her.

The fourth manner. The woman lies down, and the man lifts her legs onto his shoulders so that her buttocks no longer touch the ground. He then introduces himself to her.

The fifth manner. The woman lies on her side, and the man lies beside her, getting between her thighs so he can enter her easily. This manner is dangerous if either partner suffers from rheumatism or sciatica.

The sixth manner. The woman gets down on her knees and elbows as if kneeling for prayer. The vulva is now projecting backwards, and the man approaches from behind.

The seventh manner. The woman is on her side and the man puts one of her legs on his shoulder and the other between his thighs. Then he enters her, and can achieve movement by drawing her towards his chest with his hands, and then letting her gently fall backwards.

The eighth manner. The woman stretches herself on the ground, lying on her back with her legs crossed. The man mounts her like a cavalier on horseback.

The ninth manner. The woman is standing up, leaning forward and supporting herself on some article of furniture. The man comes to her from behind, standing up. The same manner may be achieved with both man and woman kneeling down.

The tenth manner. The woman lies back on the edge of a divan, with her legs dangling. The man lifts her legs to the height of his navel, and the woman clasps him with her legs. He then enters her and can move freely from side to side while the woman's legs still cling to him.

The eleventh manner. The woman lies back with a cushion beneath her buttocks. The man lowers himself onto her, careful to keep his weight on his hands and knees, and enters her.

This list of manners is by no means complete. Sages from different parts of the world have taught many different manners. Yet the generous man and woman, each seeking to give the greatest pleasure to the other, will discover those manners for themselves. Books cannot teach the mysteries of God, but can only give initial guidance: the individual must penetrate these mysteries for himself. Similarly books cannot teach the mysteries of love, but can only give initial guidance: if their spirit is right, the man and woman will penetrate these mysteries as they need.

Manners for Men and Women with Extreme Differences

God has not made us all the same. Some are fat and others thin. Some are tall and others short. Some have straight backs and others have crooked backs. When a man and woman meet and marry these differences are multiplied by two. The husband may be fat and the wife thin, both may be fat, both may be thin, or the husband may be thin and the wife fat. This complexity applies to the other differences. In conversation these physical differences are of no importance. But in sexual love they must be carefully taken into account.

A thin man and a fat woman. A woman may be so fat that a man cannot enter her from the front. Then he must enter her from the rear. If her fatness is due to pregnancy it is best for her to be on her side, so no pressure is put on her abdomen; she can then lift the upper thigh, and he can enter her. If her fatness is due to excessive eating, there is no danger for her in lying face downwards. They can then have union in the same way that many animals do.

A fat man and a thin woman. It is best for the woman to take the active part. Let the fat man lie on his back, with his thighs close together. The woman kneels astride him, and lowers herself onto him. She can increase the pleasure by rhythmically rising and sinking; and he can cause her to move by pressing his thighs against her buttocks. She can either sit upright, or lean forward resting her hands on the bed. If the fat man prefers that the woman lies on her back, she can part her legs, and he sits between her thighs, pushing himself into her. He may, however, find this position puts great strain on his back.

A fat man and a fat woman. In extreme cases, where both have very prominent bellies, intercourse is impossible. In less extreme cases only one manner is possible. The woman kneels, with her hands on the ground. The man approaches her from behind, resting his stomach on her posterior. However, when he becomes excited, this can put a dangerous strain on the woman's arms, which are carrying both her weight and his.

A tall man and a short woman. The problem here is to enable their sexual organs to be united and their mouths to kiss at the same time. The best way is for the woman to lie on her back, and the man lies on his side near her. He passes one of his hands under her neck, and with the other hand raises her thighs. The woman puts her arms round his neck and kisses him, while he enters her from behind. Alternatively the woman lies on her side, holding one thigh up. He inserts his body between her thighs, so that her thighs clasp his hips, while his thighs press against her buttocks. He can then enter her, and at the same time lean forward and kiss her. Much movement can be achieved if he pushes forwards and backwards, with one hand round her neck and the other on her buttocks.

A short man and a tall woman. The problem is also for their sexual organs to meet and their mouths to kiss at the same time. There are three possible manners. The first is that the woman lies on her back with a thick cushion under her buttocks and another thick cushion under her head; she draws up her thighs towards her chest. The curves in her body reduce the distance between her vulva and her mouth, enabling the man to lie on top of her, kissing her and entering her. The second is that the man and woman lie on their sides, face to face. The woman clasps the man's body with her thighs, enabling him to enter her, and clasps his neck with her arms, enabling them to kiss. The third manner is that the man lies on his back, and the woman kneels astride him; she can lean forward to kiss him, arching her back as much as necessary.

A man with a crooked back. Such a man can most conveniently enter a woman from behind. He can adopt other positions also, but unless the woman is short he will not be able to kiss her and enter her at the same time.

A woman with a crooked back. Since the woman is normally shorter than the man, a crooked back makes her so short that they will encounter the problems described earlier. There is the additional problem that she cannot lie flat on her back. It is necessary to have cushions supporting her neck and her buttocks to make intercourse possible. Sadly this restricts her movement, so the action must be entirely from the man.

These various manners of coitus devised to overcome extreme differences between the man and the woman may also be adopted by couples with no extreme difficulties, and enhance their pleasure.

It is surely a cause for wonderment that God enables problems in coitus to be turned to our advantage, allowing us to share far greater joy. This is an example of how, in God's providence, the apparent difficulties of life become channels of divine grace.

The Diverse Dances of Love

It is said that angels dance around the throne of God in heaven; and as they dance they become ecstatic with joy. If coitus is to yield ecstatic joy, it too must become a heavenly dance in which the sexual organs of the man and the woman are partners. Here are six dances that may be learnt.

The first dance is called 'the bucket in the well'. The man pushes deep into the woman, and then slowly withdraws, as if he was lifting a bucket from a well. Then the woman pushes, and slowly pulls back. They should maintain a slow, steady rhythm in their alternate movements, without any change of pace.

The second dance is called 'the mutual shock'. The man and the woman clasp each other tightly, so that he is as deep within her as possible. Then they carefully draw back, until he has almost left her; but he must be careful not to dislodge himself. They maintain this position for a few moments, and then clasp each other tightly again. This may be repeated many times.

The third dance is called 'the approach'. This is very simple and may be used to prolong coitus. The man goes into the woman very slowly: and between first entering her, and arriving deep within her, he stops five or six times, remaining completely stationary for a few moments. The movement is then repeated, but with the woman pushing. This dance requires great patience, but its rewards are also great.

The fourth dance is called 'love's tailor'. The man, when he is only just inside the woman, makes very quick, short movements, pushing inwards a short distance and then drawing back, as if he were a tailor pulling his needle quickly in and out of the cloth. This brings both the man and the woman to a peak of desire. And when they reach a peak, he plunges into the depths of her, remaining there for a time without moving. He then resumes the dance again. The danger of the dance is that it brings the man to his climax too quickly, so it is only suitable for a man with a high degree of control.

The fifth dance is called 'the toothpick'. The man enters the woman, moving in and out and from side to side with great vigour. There should be no pattern to his movements, so the woman cannot predict what he will do next. This is only suitable for a man whose sexual organ is very firm.

The sixth dance is called 'the box of love'. The man pushes so deeply into the woman that his hairs are completely intertwined with the woman's. He moves forcefully within her, without withdrawing himself at all. This dance gives the greatest pleasure of all to the woman. It may be used when the man cannot delay his climax, and thus wants to bring the woman quickly to her climax.

A man and a woman who are generous and imaginative in their love will discover variations on these dances. May God be praised for giving such a foretaste of the ecstatic dances of heaven.

The Art of Kissing

A poet once said that life itself came into being when God kissed the earth and breathed his spirit into it; and that each child is given life when an angel enters the womb to kiss the growing body within. In the same way the kiss between the man and the woman gives life to the act of love: when their mouths meet, they breathe the spirit of love into one another.

A kiss given to the outer part of the lips, making a noise similar to the one by which you call your cat, gives no pleasure. A man kisses a woman's hand in the same way as a sign of respect, not of love.

The kiss of love requires the lips to be soft and moist. If the lips are too dry, you may pass your tongue over them to make them moist. With the kiss of respect the lips stick out, and do not change shape when the two mouths meet. With the kiss of love the lips only protrude enough to invite the other's lips. Thus when the kiss begins the lips are flexible, altering their shape in response to the pressure of the kiss. This makes the saliva start to flow, and soon the sweet fresh liquid from their mouths is intermingling.

Quite naturally the man and the woman find their lips beginning to part and their mouths opening. Then their tongues should meet and caress one another. Each may also nibble the tongue of the other. Soon their tongues are performing a dance, each tongue chasing the other round the mouth.

The final stage of kissing is when the man and the woman begin to suck and drink each other's saliva. This has been compared with the camel in the desert drinking the sweet waters of an oasis. More accurately it is like drinking the finest wine, because soon the whole body and mind become intoxicated with love, and the legs and the arms begin to tremble.

Such kissing is part of the preparation for full union, fanning the flames of passion. It should also continue throughout coitus, as the manner by which the man and the woman are united allows. Indeed most couples prefer those manners of coitus which enable their sexual organs and their mouths to be united at the same time.

Some women invite their husbands to kiss them, watching the passion rise, and then refuse full coitus. Such behaviour is to be despised. It would be like God bringing life into the world, only to destroy it immediately. Just as God wants each creature to fulfil its purpose, so the union of two mouths must find fulfilment in the union of the sexual organs.

Requirements for Sexual Fulfilment

There are six things which are essential to the full joy of sexual union; and equally there are six things which can destroy that joy.

The first is bodily health. A man who is lazy, who sits all day in his house taking no exercise, has no strength for coitus. He has difficulty in achieving an erection, and even greater difficulty in maintaining it. Thus he suffers the humiliation of being unable to satisfy his wife. Young men, who still have the natural vigour of youth, can be lazy and yet be sexually successful. But do not be deceived. As the years pass and youthful vigour diminishes, so the lazy, weak man becomes impotent. It is vital, therefore, that a man maintains his bodily health by taking ample exercise each day. Then he will be able to satisfy a woman into the seventh and eighth decade of his life.

The second is health of mind. A man or a woman whose mind is filled with the cares of the world, and whose heart is heavy with anxiety, are unable to surrender themselves to passion. The flame may be ignited, but care and anxiety quickly descend upon it like a blanket, and snuff it out. It has often been said that you cannot solve a problem by worrying about it. So care and anxiety do not make a person richer or more successful, but simply destroy the pleasure and joy of life. When the husband comes to his wife, and when the wife welcomes her husband, both should learn to set aside the cares of the day, like a camel shedding its load. Then, like a camel drinking at the oasis in the cool of the evening, man and woman can drink freely at the fountain of love.

The third is a free, spontaneous heart. Many men and women feel embarrassed at letting their naked bodies be seen by their spouse, and feel guilty about sexual enjoyment. In their hearts they believe that their naked bodies are ugly, and that the pleasures of love are impure. And the guilt and embarrassment can render the woman cold and the man impotent. The root of the problem lies in the failure to link the heart with the body. Those who cannot regard sexual joy as the natural and divine expression of human love feel guilty, because for them sexual joy would indeed by impure. They must learn to understand that God has given sexual pleasure as a means by which husband and wife are bound together in love. Then with united hearts they will be able to enjoy the union of their bodies freely and without restraint.

The fourth is a natural gaiety of spirit. There are people whose spirits are locked into a dark prison of sadness and misery. Outwardly they may have every blessing that God can bestow, but inwardly they can find no light. Even kings and queens in palaces can suffer this affliction. One consequence is that there is no appetite for love. It is not easy to break out of this prison, and the only successful method is prayer. This is because those locked in the dark prison usually imagine there is some virtue in their misery, as if God himself had ordained it. In truth God wants everyone to enjoy the light of spiritual freedom, and through prayer he can make the light shine. Then the appetite for love returns.

The fifth is good food, eaten at the right time. Have meals at the same time each day, so the body is ready to digest the nourishment. Do not enjoy love immediately before a meal, as hunger for food will make you hurry the act of love. Do not enjoy love immediately after a meal, as the task of digesting the food will sap your energy. Instead enjoy love when you are neither hungry nor full, and then you will enjoy both food and sexual pleasure.

The sixth is restraint. Excessive sexual activity injures the man's health owing to the expenditure of too much sperm. Just as cream contains the essence of milk, and milk loses its quality if all the cream is skimmed off, so sperm contains the essence of a man's energy, and he will be debilitated if it is all lost. It is impossible to say how often a man should enjoy love, as this depends on his age and strength. But if a man finds that his energy is being sapped, he should practise greater restraint.

TRIBALISM

INTRODUCTION: TRIBALISM

Most religions, including almost all known tribal religions, have a creation myth, relating how the universe came into existence. And the great majority of these myths have a strong sexual element, which enables people to make sense of their sexual experiences – and also may justify the sexual customs of the society. In the Hebrew myth, told in the Book of Genesis, sexual desire between Adam and Eve is the direct consequence of their rebellion against God, which explains the guilt and shame which often surrounds sex; and yet only after the unleashing of the sexual urge does the human race begin to propagate itself, which explains the sanctity of marriage and the family. Amongst the Dogun tribe of western Sudan a sexual act was the actual agent of creation. The God of Heaven was filled with sexual desire for the Goddess of Earth and decided to have intercourse with her. The vulva of the earthly Goddess was a deep lake, and her clitoris was a termite hill on its shore. As the heavenly God descended, his divine penis erect, the termite hill also became erect, making intercourse impossible. So the God cut the huge termite hill almost to the ground, and then penetrated the lake – and as a result human and animal life was conceived. Amongst other lessons drawn from this story, it is used to justify the practice of clitoridectomy – cutting off the clitoris of pubescent girls.

The Mehinaru tribe, who live in the Amazon basin of Brazil, not only have an erotic creation myth, but have a wide range of sexual parables. They serve the estimable purpose of encouraging both men and women to be more considerate towards each other during sexual intercourse. The creation myth itself is concerned with the penis and vagina fitting well together, and implies that a young man and woman, before embarking on marriage, should ensure sexual compatability. The other stories show in the most striking manner the dire consequences of thinking only of one's own pleasure, without trying to give pleasure to one's partner.

Fertility rituals are an important element of most tribal religions, and they still find an echo in more sophisticated religious practices. Thus, for example, the Easter egg is a remnant of the fertility festival held every spring in pre-Christian Europe. Happily a most remarkable fertility song from an Australian aboriginal tribe has been written down, providing a most vivid account of the nature and meaning of their ritual. The song is used prior to the festival itself, describing what the man and woman should do. It thus serves as a form of religious sexual instruction.

Amazonian Tribe

Sensual Creation

The Divine Spirit first created men. Then he took pity on them, saying, 'They have no-one to satisfy their sexual desire.' So he made women in such a way that men could have sexual relations with them.

First he made the vagina, moulding it on a banana. Then he invited one of the men to have sex with this vagina. The man could gain no pleasure because the vagina was too big. So the Divine Spirit made another vagina with a smaller banana. Now the man could no longer insert his penis because it was too small. At last a banana the exact size of the man's penis was found, and the perfect vagina was created.

Then the Divine Spirit looked at the vagina and took pity on it, saying, 'This vagina will give no pleasure to the woman.' So he created a clitoris which, like the penis, would become erect during intercourse.

Finally the Divine Spirit fashioned a woman around the vagina, and she was the first woman in the world.

The Origin of Bananas

Long ago the Divine Spirit took the form of a handsome man. His limbs were strong and supple, his torso slim and muscular, and his penis large. He had a belt made from the finest shells around his waist, and red and yellow feathers in his hair.

He appeared by the large lake in the middle of the forest. In his deep sonorous voice he called out, 'Women of the world, come to me.' Only women could hear the call, and all the women ran from their homes to the lake. As soon as they saw him they fell in love, and forgot about their husbands. One by one he took the women in his arms and had sex with them. They had never enjoyed such pleasure, and afterwards they bowed down and worshipped him.

He ordered them not to tell their husbands what had happened, and then he sent them home. But one of the women could not keep a secret and blurted out to her husband the whole story. He was very angry. He called all the husbands together, and they marched to the lake waving their spears. When they saw the handsome man they grabbed him and pulled him to the ground. Then they cut off his penis and buried it in the ground.

At that moment the handsome man disappeared into the air. But on the spot where his penis was buried the first banana tree grew, producing the sweetest of fruits.

Sexy Worms

A woman was walking in the forest and saw a large fat worm emerging from a hole. 'It looks just like a man's penis,' she exclaimed: 'Your round head is like the head of a penis, and your mouth like a penis opening. I would like to have sex with you.' So she inserted the worm into her vagina, where it wiggled this way and that, bringing her to an orgasm. Then she took it out, and carried it home.

She hid the worm in a gourd at the back of her house, and secretly fed it porridge. Whenever her husband went out she took the worm and had sex with it. She enjoyed sex with the worm far more than sex with her husband, who would reach his climax before she was satisfied. So now she pushed her husband away when he made advances. She told all the other women in the village about her discovery, and they too went into the forest to find big, fat worms. Soon all the women were pushing away their husbands.

But one day one of the husbands came home un-expectedly, and found his wife having sex with a worm. He flew into a rage, and clubbed the worm to death. He told the other men about this, and they all clubbed their wives' worms to death.

Yet the husbands had learned a lesson. In order to retain a woman's love, a man must learn to delay his climax.

The Ring of Shells

There was once a man who had grown bored with his wife. When they had intercourse she just lay on her back without moving. And when he inserted his penis, her vagina remained motionless, giving him no pleasure. He became angry with his wife's frigidity, and she came to hate him.

One day she hatched a plan to discourage her husband from even wanting intercourse with her. She made a ring of tiny shells and put it into her vagina. 'This will cause his penis so much pain,' she said to herself, 'that he will stop coming to me and disturbing my nights.' That night her husband came to her and inserted his penis into her vagina. As his penis went through the ring of shells, a broad smile came over his face, and he cried out in delight: 'At last your vagina has learnt to grasp my penis and give me real pleasure.'

But as his penis moved this way and that within her vagina, it caused her the most terrible pain. The tiny shells scratched the inner walls of her vagina and blood poured out.

When the husband realized what had happened, he was at first angry. Then he laughed and said, 'That serves you right. Why don't you learn to have intercourse properly, so we both enjoy ourselves?'

The wife had learned her lesson. During the day she exercised the muscles of her vagina so that at night it would grip his penis firmly, giving both him and her great pleasure.

AUSTRALIAN TRIBE

Fertility Ritual

The men come, carving their wooden boomerangs.
Chips of wood fly as they march along.
They curve their boomerangs into perfect shape.
As they march their big, soft penises
Swing from side to side, and up and down.
Their penises are covered with sacred scars,
Made by the priest's knife at adolescence.
The scars are visible in the setting sun.

The women come, with wood for the fire on their heads.
They gossip and giggle as they march along.
Their happy laughter fills the air.
As they march their big, soft breasts
Swing from side to side, and up and down.
Their buttocks wobble as their legs move,
And their hips swing to the rhythm of their feet.
The men watch their moving bodies.

The women put the wood on the ground.
The men take it and build a fire.

The women now pound red ochre into dust
And rub it on their bosoms, breasts and vulvas.
The priest hands them the sacred knife,
And they shave off their pubic hairs.
The young girls who still are virgins
Put crowns of leaves on their heads.

The fire now is burning hot and bright;
All the people feel its scorching heat.
The men start walking round the fire,
And as they walk they dance.
They lift their thighs to their waists
With every step, left, right, left, right.
Then they thrust forward their hips and penises
With every step, push, push, push.

The young virgins move slowly forward
And space themselves round the men.
The men are waving their boomerangs.
They point their boomerangs at the virgins.
Then with the wooden tips they thrust,
And touch the virgins' vulvas.
The virgins cry out in searing pain,
The men cry out in intense ecstasy.

All the women now come slowly forward.
They stand stationary while the men march and dance.
Then the oldest woman gives a piercing screech,
And lunges forward to touch a man's penis.
Now all the women screech and touch,
Each grabbing the penis of a man.

The men stop and the women stroke the penises,
And soon the penises are all erect.

The men sing out a prayer to the gods,
Asking that the earth's fertility be renewed.
They pray for the soil to come back to life
And they pray for rain to feed the soil.
The women continue to stroke their penises.
The prayer of the men grows louder and louder.
The words of the prayer turn to groans and grunts.
The women sing at the tops of their voices.

Then the men's semen enters their penises,
The white liquid spurts forth into the air.
It lands on the ground and wets the earth.
The men and the women cry out together,
Praying that the semen will renew the soil.
Most men's penises now slowly subside,
But the young men's penises remain erect and potent.
They take the young virgins and enjoy them.

BIBLIOGRAPHY

Compiling this book involved using texts which were privately published and circulated, and books long out of print. Also many of the translations of ancient oriental erotic works were in Latin, rather than English, to protect the more sensitive reader. Here, however, is a list of relevant books which are reasonably accessible.

ARIEL, D., *The Mystic Quest*, Schocken Books, New York 1988.

CATULLUS, *Poems*, trans. by Frederick Raphael and Kenneth McLeish, Jonathan Cape, London 1978.

CHANG, J., *The Tao of Love and Sex*, Wildwood House 1977.

HAFIZ, *Fifty Poems* trans. A. J. Arbery, C.U.P. 1947.

HAWLEY, D. J., and JUERGGENSMEYER, M., *Songs of the Saints of India*, O.U.P. 1988.

Hindu Myths, trans. Wendy O'Flaherty, Penguin 1975.

NEFZAWI, *The Perfumed Garden* trans. Richard Burton, Grafton Books 1963.

OVID, *The Art of Love*, trans. R. Humphries, John Calder, London 1958.

RUMI, *Mystical Poems*, trans. A. J. Arberry, University of Chicago Press 1968.

STEVENS, J., *Lust for Enlightenment*, Shambhala 1990.

VATSYAYANA, *Kama Sutra*, trans. R. Burton and F. F. Arbuthnot, Mandala 1965.

VANN, G., *To Heaven with Diana*, Collins 1960.

VIDYAPATI, *Love Songs*, trans. D. Bhattacharya, George Allen and Unwin, London 1963.